Last Train to St. Kilda?
By Paul Davies

Script Paul Davies
Photographs Ruth Maddison
Drawings Barry Dickens
Director Dennis Moore
Stage Design Greg Carroll
Lighting Design Liz Pain
Costume Design Susan Weiss
Original Music Tony Leonard
Graphics Michael Trudgeon

Bringing the World
Back Together

A Picture Play

ACKNOWLEGEMENTS

My deepest, heartfelt gratitude to all those made this play both possible and necessary. To Caz and Tabby who inspired it. To my father to paid some of the bills. To the painter Paul Cavell who gave it it's first title ("Hullo Cockie" in 1974). To TheatreWorks (past and present) who created the physical circumstances for it to happen in. And finally to all those many theatrical magicians (Wolfgang, Dennis, Cast and Crew) who risked their very considerable reputations in order to be associated with it. To all of you, thank you…

Theatre is the ultimate community. The price of Liberty is Eternal Vigilance.

First Produced by TheatreWorks
August 4 to 31, 1987

All rights by all media reserved.
(Private & Confidential)
(c) Paul Davies
The moral authority of the author has been asserted.

Barry Dickens drawings appeared as slides throughout the performance.

This book is copyright. Apart from any fair dealing for the purpose of private study, research or review, as permitted under the Copyright Act, no part may be reproduced by any process without written permission. Inquiries concerning publication, performance translation or recording rights should be addressed to the author Any performance or public reading of *Last Train To St. Kilda* requires a license from the author. The purchase of this book in no way gives the purchaser the right to perform the play in public, whether by means of a staged production or a reading.

© The moral right of the author has been asserted.

CONTENTS

Cast	5
Writer's Notes (1987)	7
Writer's Notes (2019)	9
Last Train To St. Kilda?	
ACT 1	13
ACT 2	113
Critical Reception	193
Programme Materials	225
Author	229
Dedication	231

CAST

L-R: Jean Kittson, Helen Tripp, Paul Davies, Caz Howard, Rod Williams

JOHN A. SMITH. (Paul Davies)
Late thirties, assistant junior manager at Colesworth's Supermarket, regards himself as basically a responsible, decent, ordinary working bloke.

SUZI WISEMAN. (Caz Howard)
Bank teller, early thirties, disciplined and pragmatic champion of people's rights and freedoms (especially her own), health and fitness conscious.

COLLEEN O'NEILL (Jean Kittson)
St. Kilda barmaid, early thirties, a struggling, hardworking, open minded graduate of the university of hard knocks.

NORM (Rod Williams) and **DOTTY** (Helen Tripp) **DRINKWATER**
Late forties, perhaps even early fifties, a "semi-retired" couple, came to St. Kilda for a two week holiday 30 years ago, rising lower middle or lower upper under class. In other words they're moderately well off. But not very.

The actors also play other characters:

Jean Kittson: COLLEEN O'NEIL (also AUCTIONEER, CONSTABLE HANDLING, INSURANCE AGENT, PIZZA DELIVERY GIRL, INSPECTOR RAMSHOTT)

Helen Tripp: DOTTY DRINKWATER (also BAG LADY, BERYL, ESTER HAZY, NIGHT CLUB SINGER, COMMUTER, SOCIAL WORKER, CONSTANBLE MCKEAN)

Roderick Williams: NORM DRINKWATER (also HARRY THE BROOM, BANK MANAGER, SGT. PRIMUS, THE FERRET, WAITER, STATION MASTER)

Caz Howard: SUZI WISEMAN (also the SPIRIT OF ST. KILDA

Paul Davies: JOHN A SMITH (also SPY AT PUBLIC RALLY)

WRITER'S NOTES (1987)

On the 13th of May 1857 the first train to St. Kilda ran on a line that was built amid great controversy. South Melbourne residents fiercely objected to the closure of their streets and the brawling finally stopped when both sides realized that only their lawyers were getting rich.

On the 31st of July 1987 (four days before this play opens) the last train will run on the St. Kilda line amidst great controversy. Local residents are objecting to the closure of their transport options. By all accounts the fighting will continue.

For 130 years Australia's oldest passenger train got people from the centre of Melbourne to St. Kilda in nine minutes. With current traffic congestion levels still increasing it will soon take a number of hours by car. It used to cost 9 pence for a 16 hour ticket. It will soon cost a fortune in petrol, insurance, lead pollution and road trauma.

Can this be called "progress"?

The coming of the railway line transformed a sleepy bayside village full of wealthy merchants, squatters and retired sea captains into one of the most famous destinations in the country. On swelteringly hot February Sundays thousands of people surged through the St Kilda station's turnstiles. The aristocratic, seaside playground became a refuge and relief for the factory workers of Fitzroy, Richmond and Collingwood. Now the removal of the line comes at a time when St. Kilda is again going through extraordinary changes. But into what? And for whom?

This play started life as a story called "Invasion of Privacy" in which two loving optimists, looking for a more tolerant and vibrant community, arrive in St. Kilda and are burgled almost immediately. They were driven slowly crazy by a constant and irresistible assault on their personal life. But is privacy possible? Or even a good thing?

We are entering a society where we will soon be known, not by our names, but by our numbers – where public information resides in fewer and fewer private hands, where private transport produces a greater loneliness, and where six foot high fences keep our neighbours out but burglars in.

This is a play about the oldest railway line in Australia, but it is not a play about the past. It's a dream about a possible future – about the transformation of a community and perhaps the erosion of the idea of "community" itself.

But can an individual turn the tide? Can a play save a railway line? Will the lights work tonight? Have the costumes come back from the dry cleaners? Could the cast turn up sober? The trains may have stopped but they're not gone forever.

WRITER'S NOTES (2019)

Last Train to St. Kilda? was the fourth of six plays I wrote for TheatreWorks and by any measure it was the least successful. A planned five week season (with a possible fortnight's extension) was cut back to just one month of performances. While the house numbers seemed modest but reasonable at the time, the audience response at the end of some performances of the play was distinctly muted. Not good for a playwright standing behind the curtain with his dispirited cast, pondering the ominous silence on the other side. One critic made a somewhat noisy exit about ten minutes into opening night, pretty much voting with his feet. Certain theatre colleagues, directors and actors, quietly confessed to me afterwards that it "wasn't their cup of tea". Since I also played the main character of John Smith it became somewhat personally challenging to keep going on.

Most critics found that the problem lay principally with the script. I remember even writing back to *The Australian* requesting a second opinion on that, given the negativity of their critic, Helen Thompson's demolition job. I guess my febrile attempt to channel Kafka and Orwell through a Joe Orton-esque black comedy failed to cut the mustard for the critical establishment. And for several decades I have buried the play in a bottom drawer at home, thinking, well - nice try but no cigar. Certainly I never kept anything like the extensive archives I held on other, more successful plays. It was indeed a stroke of good luck that Ruth Madison had kept her production stills because I had almost nothing in the file.

Reading it again 32 years later for the purposes of publishing it here with Ruth's photographs and Barry Dickens images, I'm not quite so embarrassed. Parts of it I feel are a lot better than I recall. The attempt wasn't just to protest the closing of the oldest rail line in Australia (the play opened four days after the actual closure in July 1987) but to reflect on the changing demographics of St. Kilda and what this process of rapid gentrification meant for the community living there, And indeed TheatreWorks move to St. Kilda was emblematic of that process of change. Much of the play *is* personal. Caz Howard and I were burgled twice straight after moving into 27 Fawkner Street, and TheatreWorks itself had the box office takings stolen (about $400) on the first night in our new theatre when the front of house person had to go inside to do the lights. So I wasn't exaggerating about the extent of petty crime involved in the suburb. We'd come from the Eastern suburbs and this was our wake up call. Here was a different set of rules.

Perhaps the real problem with the script lay in the fact that there was no real happy, or even uplifting ending. For critics and some audiences the play seemed too episodic, a series of bleak situations tumbling one after the other and not adding up to very much. Humour is a funny thing (pun intended). What works for some doesn't necessarily work for others. Nevertheless the A list critics were fairly unanimous. Helen Thompson while starting out with a positive look back at earlier plays of mine, found *Last Train* "seriously flawed" – both in its writing and production. For her the plot was simple and the characters "crude stereotypes with about as much complexity as a comic strip." The police were "gun happy fools persecuting the innocent and failing to deal with the criminals". But in fact that's the response Caz and I actually *did* experience with the police after our own burglaries on arrival in St. KIlda. They even told us which pub in Port Melbourne we could probably buy our stolen goods back from. But Helen Thompson found the result "confused" and that it "failed to demonstrate a real alternative to the ills it deplores" assuming that theatre has this social and moral imperative.

Melbourne's most influential critic, Leonard Radic (*The Age*) while also impressed by my earlier work on trams and boats and in houses, found *Last Train* "thin and dramatically undernourished". For Radic the play was "strong on humour but weak on sociology and analysis." Likewise, Barry Oakley (*Times on Sunday*) found that while there were some "funny and telling moments" the "writing is uneven, the structure shaky and the scenes follow one another jerkily". Chris Boyd, syndicated across a number of community papers, concluded that while there were "some brilliant ideas and razor sharp observations… for each classic line (however) there are a dozen clichés." For Boyd the "sum was less than the parts" but he also conceded that it might appeal to "lovers of farce or activists who need some comic relief."

John Hindle (*Melbourne* Herald) while generally positive, found the characters "likeable" and the experience a "pleasant, (albeit) slight evening of humour and social satire". Geoffrey Milne (*Centre Stage*) called the play a "whacky look at what St. Kilda (and the nation) might be in a decade's time". But while this was for Milne "a very funny piece well served by Dennis Moore's inventive and energetic production and a good cast" nevertheless, he felt that problems with the play's "awkward structure" and its "tendency to take on more themes and issues than it can develop render it an enjoyable, punchy, vigorous but ultimately evanescent piece".

On a more positive note Ann Nugent (*Canberra Times*) found the play "entertaining" and felt it was great to be "in a community theatre packed to capacity (about 300) by and appreciative and theatre wise audience". And, saving the best for last, the most positive of all came from the critic for the *Toorak Times* who called the show "inventive" ,"highly original" and the "funniest night's entertainment seen on stage in Melbourne for years." "The laughs come thick and fast". In fact for this critic the play was "so good one wonders how long it will be before his (Davies') material enters the mainstream theatre, perhaps the MTC."

Alas, the call from the MTC never came and my material never did quite make into the mainstream…

Somewhere in the near FUTURE........

1. ST KILDA STATION   NIGHT/DAWN (1999)
JOHN A. SMITH, OLD STATION MASTER (Rod Williams),
HOMELESS LADY (Helen Tripp),

A gloomy light fades up revealing: St. Kilda Station. An end point on the old Melbourne – St. Kilda railway line. The station is currently (in 1999) a depressing collection of ramshackle sheds.

Somewhere off a SAX PLAYING BUSKER sets a bluesy, big-city mood. It is the dead of night sometime in the near future…

Gradually we become aware of an approaching rattle of bottles and soon a derelict looking man (JOHN), dressed in a black duffle coat and odd fitting boots pushes a pram-full of sorted garbage along the railway line.

He slows as he passes a Metrail rubbish bin, just on the edge of a pool of light cast from the nearby station platform. He sneaks a quick look into the bin, nonchalantly scattering a few plastic bags on its surface.

Suddenly he stops and steps back again. There's somebody asleep on one of the station benches, huddled under an old army great coat. JOHN looks…

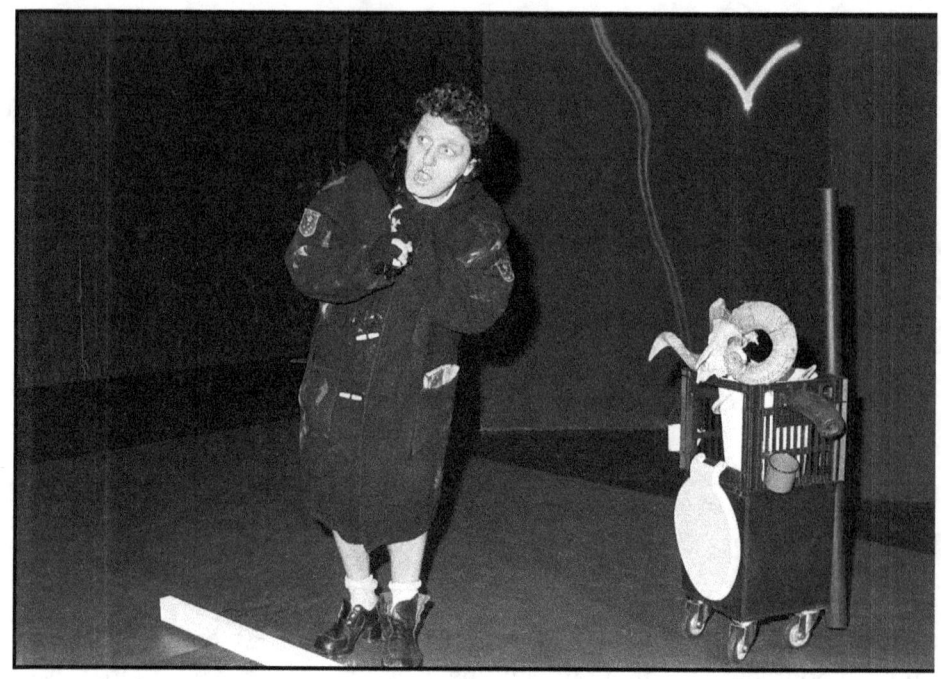

JOHN. Oh god! What am I doing ?

The stubbie falls from his hands as he turns away from THE BAG LADY, mortified.

He clambers up onto the platform and sinks onto the bench beside her.

>JOHN. You see what happens when you lose your Australia card !
>I didn't' mean to put the thing in an autobank machine. I was in a hurry. I needed money. I fumbled my wallet! I made a mistake. !
>Jesus ! I'm sorry !

The memory of it rekindles his frustrations, he climbs back to his feet, shaking an angry fist at the indifferent stars above.

>JOHN. Is it my fault they're the same shape and size as a bloody bankcard ! I've always tried to do the right thing. Always. But what's

> the point, eh ? About the only thing I've got left is this
> cold sore, and all I'm allowed to buy is a cheap,
> two dollar copy of the "*Daily Liar*".

He finds a copy of the paper amongst the rubbish and hurls it angrily away into the darkness.

> JOHN. I was junior assistant sub-manager at a
> very respectable supermarket. I had a
> mortgage. I ordered people around. I even
> voted for the Liberal Party! (jumps down onto
> the tracks again)
> I could have *amounted to something* !

He sinks to his knees on the bare sleepers.

> JOHN. Life's a bitch and then you die. So
> bugger it. And you can quote me on that.

He stretches out across the line, his head resting on one rail, his foot pawing out to reach the other. Then he lies back and tries to simply go to sleep.

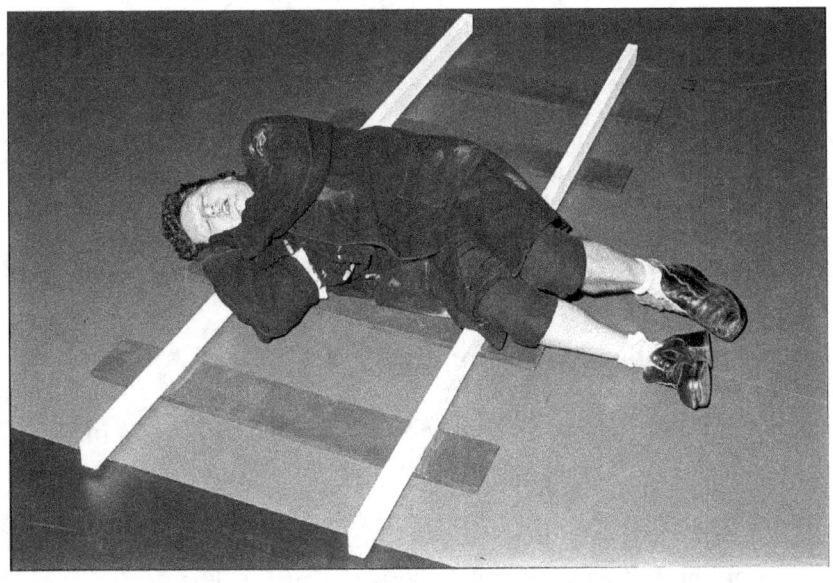

JOHN. Oh yes. Those were his last words: "Bugger it."

Finally he gives up wriggling, trying to stretch himself out longer across the track and leaps to his feet.

JOHN. And bugger this frigging railway line !
How am I supposed to kill myself on
something that's nearly as wide as I am ? Jesus !

He kicks at the solid steal track but only succeeds in hurting his foot.

JOHN. (hopping on one leg, GROANING)
Bloody Victoria, it - would have to have the
widest railway gauge in the whole frigging
country !

He looks quickly up the track in both directions.

JOHN. They never come when you want 'em
do they ? (bending down to THE BAG
LADY). Still - don't let my death upset your
day, eh ? You just lie there and have a good
night out. It's no sweat off your nose if I'm ...
squashed to death is it?

He subsides back down again but a steel railway line is not such a comfortable pillow. First he lies on his side in a foetal position, then he turns over to the other side. He slaps the rail, SIGHING.

JOHN. Well, I'm happy to go to sleep but I'm
not going
to go out un-bloody-comfortable.

He reaches up and pulls a tatty air mattress out of his pram, starts blowing it up.

JOHN. (almost hyperventilating) Great way to
get high, this you know. (between puffs). The
poor man's stone. Wanta, feel spaced out ?

> (going cress-eyed) Blow an air mattress up. Works
> every time... Doesn't cost...a ...cent (losing
> his breath).

His talk fades as the effort of blowing defeats-him. He starts to stagger on his feet a little, becoming dizzy.

> JOHN. Wow. (shakes his head) Nothing like
> one last hit before you go...

He collapses down on the half blown-up air mattress and passes out on the sleepers. Soon he's SNORING.

Gradually THE SKY BRIGHTENS.

Birds begin to TWITTER in the gum trees beside the line.

The former STATION MASTER (now known as "HARRY THE BROOM" because of his cleaning job) enters onto the platform pushing two white Council bins on a kind of billycart made from old packing cases and bicycle wheels. Large brooms are wedged in between the bins. "National Trust" is stenciled on the back of his white overalls. He starts picking up JOHN'S rubbish, scattered about earlier, then double takes and starts leaning over the edge of the platform, calling down to him.

> HARRY. Hey, mate ! You tryin' to kill
> yourself ? (CHUCKLES)
>
> JOHN. (stirring awake) Let me die in peace
> will you.
>
> HARRY. You lucky bastard.
>
> JOHN. Oh bugger off !
>
> HARRY. This is the old St. Kilda line, mate.
>
> JOHN. (indignantly) I know that !

HARRY. Well, the St. Kilda line's been closed for thirteen
years.

JOHN frowns at HARRY, not too sure of his ground.

JOHN. Thirteen years ?

HARRY sinks down to his knees down beside JOHN, almost reverential.

HARRY. This is New Year's eve, mate, 1999. We've just about to enter a new millennium.

JOHN. Well, I'm trying to enter heaven, if you don't mind.

HARRY. You lucky, lucky bastard. 'Wish I could give it all away that easily (stretching out, resting his head back on the palms of his hands, mimicking JOHN's posture). But the stars, eh ? (gazing up at them) And all that endless blue sky… Makes you think, doesn't it ? Could we be the only intelligent life in all that vast cosmos ? Seems unlikely, but what if we were… how extraordinary… Maybe, maybe we only exist so that the universe can become conscious of itself. (thinks about his idea, likes it, nods) We are the instrument by which the cosmos gets to know itself… (carried away by his insight)

JOHN (cutting in, sitting up) Look ! This is my suicide, do you mind ?
I'm utterly miserable.

HARRY. Don't knock misery, mate. People love to see other people worse off than themselves. That's why they watch so much TV News.

JOHN. (intense frustration) Oh Christ !

HARRY. I'm the one who oughta kill meself. My life's had more ups and downs than a bride's nightie … I used to be the Station Master here.

It finally hits JOHN.

JOHN. But - they can't have closed it down ! This was the oldest railway line in Australia.

HARRY. Passenger line. Oldest *passenger* line.

He reaches into one of his bins (which is really a giant esky) and rummages around inside it.

HARRY. Port Melbourne was actually the original Australian railway line. That's a congested freeway and open sewer now.

Finally locating what he's after HARRY pulls out two stubbies of beer, handing one to JOHN.

> JOHN. (taking a beer) Thanks very much.
>
> HARRY. (clinking tins) Happy 2000.
>
> JOHN. Cheers

They drink.

> HARRY. Yep. for 130 years people got from St. Kilda to the city in 9 minutes.
>
> JOHN. (glumly) Takes hours by car now.
>
> HARRY. I know, I know, quicker to walk. But …

HARRY quickly drains his stubbie and reaches in for another one.

> HARRY. As my old man used to say: "let's live a little". (drinks again, then realises) Oh- sorry… .
>
> JOHN. That's OK.
>
> HARRY. No, no here I am, barging into your private moment. Blatherin' on about the golden past.
>
> JOHN. Look, I appreciate it, really… I… I had no idea - about the line you know.

He looks up and down the tracks, shakes his head.

> JOHN. It's funny really I remember the first trip I ever took to St. Kilda. Must have been over a decade ago…

CUT TO:

2. EXT./INT. TRAIN TRAVELLING DAY   DAY (1987)
JOHN, SUZI, COLLEEN, MALE COMMUTER (Rod Williams)
HOMELESS LADY (Helen Tripp)

>VOICE OVER (PA) Flinders Street. Flinders Street, Platform 11. St. Kilda Train. Departing now. (A BELL RINGS) Stand clear please Stand clear…

There's a WHISTLE from the guard's cabin, and an ANSWERING TOOT
from the driver and slowly the "toot" and the "whistle" establish a relentless musical theme.

Everybody on board the train shakes in rhythm to its movement. Carried by the MUSIC.

It is obviously a crowded, peak hour time. JOHN and SUZI enter, squeezing past people.

>SUZI. I don't like St. Kilda. I don't like the idea of it.
>
>JOHN. Idea of it?

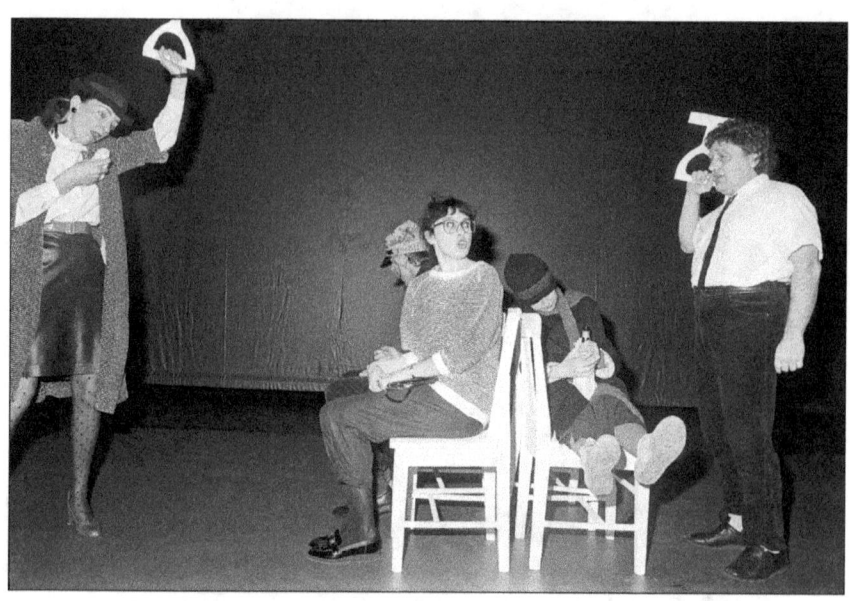

SUZI. I don't like the people you see in the street. You can't trust anybody.

JOHN (looking around, suspiciously) Trust anybody ?

He squeezes past COLLEEN to be confronted by a SLEEPING DERRO sprawled across the only available seat. Meanwhile SUZI slides easily into the seat beside a MALE COMMUTER.

JOHN. What's that got to do with it ? At least in St. Kilda people are more tolerant. (abruptly shaking the DERRO'S leg, trying to wake her up) You can be eccentric. It doesn't matter.

JOHN finally gives up the "gentle" approach and quite rudely swings the DERRO'S feet off the seat. This has the effect of sweeping her straight up into a sitting position, leaving her wondering why she's suddenly awake, and wishing she wasn't, and why is she holding this brown paper bag with the open bottle of port in it ?

SUZI. Eccentric ! You're not planning to go eccentric on me are you, John ?

She makes it sound like a contagious disease. JOHN feels distinctly hemmed in by the DERRO. He's squeezed in beside her and now has his back to SUZI.

> JOHN. But Fitzroy and Brunswick are so crowded, landlocked. I couldn't breathe there (fanning a bad smell away). Think of the lead levels. Come on - you're the health fanatic.
>
> SUZI. But all my friends live within a short walk of Brunswick St.
>
> JOHN. And that doesn't *worry* you fercrissake !

For some reason the DERRO keeps trying to take the brown paper bag off her bottle over and over - but can't physically or intellectually muster the wherewithall to quite manage it.

Meanwhile. Sitting beside SUZI the MALE COMMUTER goes through the strangely elaborate ritual of "commuter macramé" - that folding of newspapers into extremely narrow columns in order to facilitate their being read in crowded and awkward spaces. SUZI baulks at this routine for a moment.

> JOHN. (pleading, reasonable) Think of the beach, Sooz,
> Summer. We can go for a swim at the end of our street.
>
> SUZI. I'd want a second opinion on that.
>
> JOHN. There's always a sea breeze.
>
> SUZI. Sea *gale* more like it.
>
> JOHN. Even better, pure air, Sooz. Pure unpolluted Southern Hemisphere air.

SUZI. Yeah, coming straight off Antarctica.

John sighs. Slumps.

JOHN. I think you're being unreasonable.

SUZI. If this house is no good we're definitely going to look in Brunswick next Saturday.

We hear the CLANGING OF BELLS from the railway level crossing go past.
RED FLASHING LIGHTS flood the train.

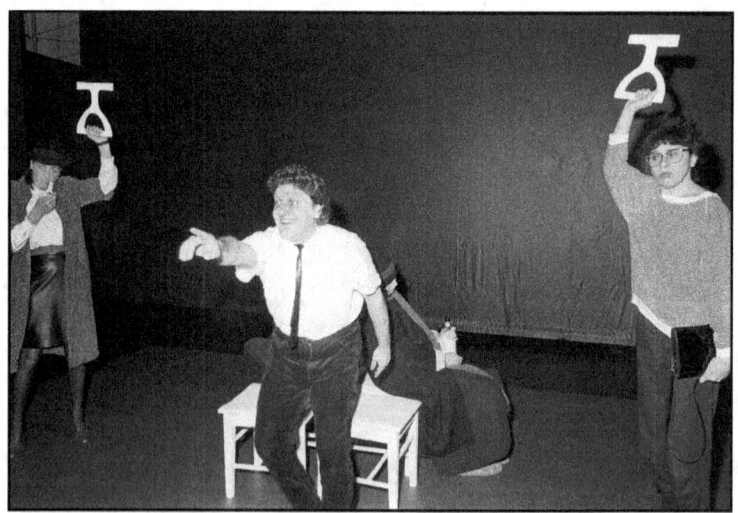

JOHN. (pointing out the window) There it *is*, Sooz, there's our little home!

Excited, JOHN leaps to his feet - and straight into the underarm of COLLEEN.

He reels back from the collision, suffering a slight delayed reaction.

>COLLEEN. Aw sorry, mate.

>JOHN. (shrugs; holding the bridge of his nose)
>That s OK - it's just a bit wet.

>BLACKOUT.

3. ADJOINING BACKYARDS   DAY (1987)
JOHN, SUZI, AUCTIONEER (Jean Kittson) NORM, DOTTY, FERRET (Rod Williams)

The BELLS of the level crossing cross fade to the sound of the AUCTIONEER'S BELL. During the change, slides of houses with big "For Sale" signs flash across the screen. Toecutter & Lebensraum Agents.

SPOTLIGHT on the AUCTIONEER, holding her hammer, ready to slam it down…

AUCTIONEER. And what a fantastic little bargain we've got for you here today, ladies and gentlemen. We've got the Big Four "P"s. We've got: Position, Popularity, Proximity to shops, schools and transport, and most of all we've got - Price. You don't have to be an Einstein to realize what an extraordinary transformation St. Kilda is going through today. So get in on the ground floor of a real estate boom. Nobody will be disappointed with 27 Batman Street, ladies and gentlemen. The first to inspect will say "Buy ! Buy ! Buy !

The LIGHTS COME UP on an incredibly ramshackle backyard, strewn with rubbish. As SUZI and JOHN wander in for their inspection.

SUZI. This place is a dump.

JOHN. Well you can see it's been lived in.

SUZI. Lived in ! Who by ? The Hell's Angels ?

JOHN. Look, at least it hasn't just been done up for some quick sale. There's no cosmetic paint job to hide all the flaws.

SUZI. I don't think any paint job could.

JOHN. God! You're really blocking, today.

SUZI. Well, I'm used to living alone.

JOHN sighs.

JOHN. You don't live alone, you've got a place with Sky and Tobsha.

SUZI. I just don't know if I'm ready for something permanent yet.

JOHN. Christ ! It's a great time to have second thoughts.

JOHN kicks a rusty can of Coke flying, they stand with their backs to each other as the LIGHTS COME ON in the adjoining yard.

Next door, the DRINKWATERS (NORM and DOTTY) are huddled next to the fence on their side, crouching behind it. Listening in.

DOTTY holds a compact mirror up - just above the fence line and pretends to be putting on lipstick while actually spying on JOHN and SUZI, using the mirror like a periscope.

From this first moment you see him and all throughout the play, NORM is constantly holding a can of beer and puffing on a fag. DOTTY, for her part is the full suburban housewife nightmare: fluffy moccasins and hair in rollers.

>NORM. Come on Dot, what do you reckon ?

>DOTTY. Well, he looks like a sort of burnt out junior supermarket Manager. And she looks like a bank clerk.

>NORM. (thoughtfully) Mmm. This mob'll be harder to bounce.

For the first time DOTTY actually notices her face in the mirror. She's managed to smudge lipstick virtually everywhere but on her lips.

Meanwhile, JOHN and SUZI are moving out of the backyard towards the audience. SUZI pauses to regard the house, somewhat critically - from the railway line.

SUZI. (cranes he neck to one side) That house has got a distinct lean to it.

JOHN. (giving up) Oh well we might just as well start looking in Clayton then.

SUZI. What - the suburb you live in when you're not actually alive ?

JOHN. (putting his foot down) There's nothing else I've seen as good
as this within our price range. This is what you get for fifty seven/ sixty thousand dollars these days.

They move on into the audience, who now effectively operate as potential buyers at an auction. Meanwhile, NORM transforms into THE FERRET and quietly slips into the back of the CROWD (audience).

SUZI. Yeah, but will they take fifty seven thousand ?

JOHN. (senses that she's, wavering) You'll never get these prices in St. Kilda again.

SUZI. I want a second opinion on that.

JOHN. I mean it's not as if we're getting married or anything .

SUZI. Isn't it ?

JOHN. We're simply buying a house together, that's all. Taking control of our lives for a change.

SUZI. By going into debt ?

The AUCTIONEER comes forward takes up a megaphone.

AUCTIONEER. Before I place myself in your hands ladies and gentlemen are there any questions concerning this splendid renovator's opportunity at 27 Batman Street ?

SUZI stands

SUZI. I'd just like to ask about the railway line.

AUCTIONEER. (cheerfully) Yes madam ?

SUZI. Well, it's a bit close isn't it ?

AUCTIONEER. (chuckles) This is the St. Kilda line, madam. You'd be surprised how few trains go past here.

SUZI. Still, they're pretty noisy.

JOHN. (trying to tug her down) So--oz !

AUCTIONEER. I don't think you'll need to worry about the
railway line too much longer madam. (turning back to the CROWD)
So - ladies and gentlemen, it's over to you and as the judge said to the chorus girl "I'm in your hands, now my dear, make me offer I can't refuse…

SILENCE for a moment.

JOHN. (tentatively, clearing his throat) Ah – thirty eight thousand dollars. . .

The AUCTIONEER LAUGHS.

32

> AUCTIONEER. Well - alright, just for a laugh, I'll start at thirty eight and take rises of ten. Do I hear 48 ?

The FERRET raises his hand.

> AUCTIONEER. Thank you sir, that's 48 thousand. I've got 48…48,
>
> JOHN. 58
>
> AUCTIONEER. (to the FERRET) And against you sir.
>
> FERRET. 68

JOHN looks disappointed and slightly downcast. This is going to be hard.

> AUCTIONEER. At 68 thousand dollars what a bargain this would be!

JOHN summons some courage and raises his hand.

JOHN. 78.

SUZI. (restraining) John –

AUCTIONEER. Thank you sir, and against you again, sir. (pointing her hammer at the FERRET)

FERRET. 88.

SUZI. (relieved, pleased) That's it John, we're going.

JOHN. (tentative hand up) Will you take rises of 5 ?

AUCTIONEER. Thank you sir, that's 93 thousand. I'm looking for 98.

JOHN. Oh, no, no, I (didn't mean to bid…just…asked a)

AUCTIONEER. 98 thousand 98. Do I hear 103 ?

SUZI. John, will you sit down and shut-up!

JOHN. (to SUZI) I wasn't bidding that time, it's a mistake,
I just asked her if she'd "take another 5…"

AUCTIONEER. And - another 5 thousand, thank you sir.

JOHN. NO!

SUZI. Christ!

AUCTIONEER. 103. I now have 103 thousand Australian *doulers*, (punning in French) and let's face it they're not worth all that much these days are they ?

JOHN. Look, excuse me (putting up his hand, tentative).

AUCTIONEER. And another 5 makes it 108. (turning to the FERRET) And it's against you, sir… I'm looking for 113, 113 thousand dollars.

The FERRET shakes his head. Looking despondent. Then slicks into the background…

JOHN. There's been a mistake !

AUCTIONEER. A real give-away at 113 thousand dollars…(raising her hammer to count it down)

JOHN turns anxiously to the CROWD around him.

JOHN. Oh come on somebody, it… it's worth a lot more than that!

SUZI. (through gritted teeth) John, *ferchrissake* !

JOHN (trying to lift the arm of an audience member sitting next to him) 113 ! Go on 113… (urging them to bid)

He becomes increasingly desperate and frantic. (If the audience actually joins in and starts bidding it keeps going so that JOHN always ends up with the last bid)

SUZI (practically screaming at him, restraining him physically)

John !

AUCTIONEER. Thank you, John. 113, I have 113.

JOHN. No! No- not me ! Him ! Him! (or Her ! Her !)
(pointing to the relevant audience member)

AUCTIONEER. Are you all said ? Are you all done ? Going once.
(hammer into palm)

JOHN. NO!

AUCTIONEER. Going twice.
(second hammer into palm)

JOHN. Wait. Wait!

AUCTIONEER. Going three times. (she hits the lectern with her gavel) And congratulations, sir, on a very fine purchase indeed.

Next door NORM and DOTTY are ecstatic. This means their home is worth five times what they paid for it.

DOTTY. Oh Norm !

NORM. Yes !

BLACKOUT on the Auctioneer.

Lights stay on THE AUDIENCE and the newly acquired backyard of 13 Batman Street.

APPLAUSE breaks out.

JOHN'S mouth drops open, he looks stunned.

Beside him SUZI is equally aghast.

SILENCE for a few moments.

>SUZI. I feel sick..

Something in JOHN snaps, he rounds on THE AUDIENCE, eye's aflame, flinging off his coat.

>JOHN (blaming them) You utter, utter BASTARDS !!!!

>SUZI. Oh sit down and shut-up!

JOHN'S eyes take on a distant look, he sinks into his chair.

>JOHN. I suppose I ... I could ... always sell my scooter.

>SUZI. This is an unmitigated disaster, my life is ruined !.

SUZI gives up, detaches herself from the audience and staggers back across the railway line into the backyard. Stands there holding herself in sick to the stomach.

>JOHN. (meekly following her, emotionally exhausted) Did you. . . (stops listens for something) Did the hammering of her gavel remind you of anything?

>SUZI. Yes - the nails in my coffin !

>JOHN. No - No I mean the silence. At least we've got that much, darling. At least we've got peace and quiet.

Immediately he says it there's an incredible CLANGING OF BELLS from the nearby level crossing gates. A FLASHING RED LIGHT again bathes the set, followed by the enormous din of a TRAIN CRASHING PAST.

CUT TO

4. INT. BANK   **DAY (1987)**
SUZI, JOHN, BANK MANAGER (Rod Williams), BAG LADY (Helen Tripp), COLLEEN (Jean Kittson)

The BELLS of the level crossing carry over into the BELLS of a telephone RINGING somewhere in the offices of a small suburban bank - that incessant, annoying RINGING PHONE that no one seems prepared to answer.

Slides establish that this is the public, counter area of a branch of the "Jap-Hand Australasian Bank"

SUZI is at her job as a teller, standing behind the counter. An old BAG LADY is shouting at her through thick bullet proof glass of SUZI's cashier's window.

> BAG LADY. No. No. Cheltenham. Cheltenham. It's me pension cheque, you know. I'm on the snag.
>
> SUZI. Yeah, well you can't cash it here.

BAG LADY. (hard of hearing – peeling an ear forward) What ?

SUZI. (shouting back, spelling it out) You. Can't. Cash. It. Here!

BAG LADY. Why not ?

SUZI (opening her bullet proof Window). You. Have. To. Go. To. Your. Local. Branch.

BAG LADY. But I always cash it today. What is it ? Thursday ? Friday?

SUZI. It's Monday ! (swinging around to an unseen teller behind her) Ray will you answer the bloody phone !

COLLEEN O'NEILL enters, looking very glamorous in fur coat, stiletto heels, and carrying an expensive leather briefcase. She waits behind the BAGLADY.

BAG LADY. I can't go back to Cheltenham, love, I haven't got the fare. That's why I wanted to cash me cheque here.

The phone keeps RINGING. So the BAG LADY backs off, uncertain. COLLEEN slides past her to take her place at the window opposite SUZI.

SUZI. Ray -

COLLEEN proceeds to unlock her briefcase and unload several thick wads of $100 notes (all with curious holes drilled through them) SUZI starts counting COLLEEN'S money.

BAG LADY. I want to see the manager!

SUZI. Mr. Hendrix is out at the moment.

Suddenly JOHN enters. wearing a black menacing looking bike helmet, black jacket and thick leather gloves, he carries a musical instrument case under one arm.

SUZI takes one look at him and screams which is echoed by the other two women who immediately hit the floor.

ALARM BELLS add to the cacophony. There's general panic !

>JOHN. Sooz, Sooz, it's me ! John.

He takes his helmet off, SUZI relaxes.

>JOHN. (holding his helmet, sheepishly) Sorry.

The alarm stops just as the MANAGER pokes his head in from a rear office.

>MANAGER. What in the blazes is going on ?

>SUZI. (casting a despairing look at JOHN) It's just your 11 o'clock appointment, Mr. Hendrix.

>MANAGER. Well, I don't need a major crime alert to remind me Miss Wiseman. (staring darkly at her)

She lets JOHN in past the counter and he follows the MANAGER into a back office. SUZI snatches the instrument case off him as he pushes past her.

>BAG LADY. (pointing towards Managers Office) Here, I thought you said he was out.

>BLACKOUT on the public counter area.

LIGHTS UP on the MANAGER'S OFFICE:

The MANAGER settles comfortably into his executive style chair and as he does so we notice that it's a good foot or so higher than the child-like stool that John tentatively shambles into on the opposite side of the desk.

This physical enhancement of John's low status does little for his nerves of pure marshmallow. His head barely reaches above the line of the desk.

>MANAGER. Well, ah … ah… (holding out his hand while simultaneously scanning his appointments diary for a name)
>
>JOHN. John. John A. Smith.
>
>MANAGER. John. Fred Hendrix. (shakes hands still without looking at him)

Then finally looks up.

MANAGER. What can JapHand Australasian do for you?

JOHN. Well, to be perfectly frank, Fred, I'm feeling about as frivolous as a fat frog in a French Restaurant.

MANAGER. Fascinating. What's the prognosis ?

JOHN. I'm fucked. (simply)

MANAGER Fine. Did it happen in the normal intercourse of events ?

JOHN grips the edge of the Manager's desk, squeezing it nervously swaying slightly at the horrendous memory of it all.

JOHN. Actually it happened quite simply.

Suddenly a bit of the manager's desk top comes away in JOHN'S hand. He looks shocked, tries to stick it back on - hopelessly.

JOHN. Sorry -

MANAGER. That's alright.

So JOHN sort of tentatively rests the broken-off bit on top of the rest of the desk. The MANAGER ignores it, waiting for him to go on.

JOHN. You see, sir, I did a pretty silly thing on the weekend. (his bottom lip trembling) I went and bought a house! (bursts out SOBBING)

MANAGER. (sympathetic) There… there… (gives him a hankie)

JOHN. Ta (JOHN sniffles into it)

MANAGER. I've only used a corner.

JOHN baulks at that, but continues and dabs at his eyes. The MANAGER settles back in his chair. Relaxed

>MANAGER. That's not a silly thing to do, John.
>
>JOHN. (weakly through his sobs) It isn't it ? (a glimmer of hope)
>
>MANAGER. No, son, no. That's a perfectly normal, perfectly Australasian thing to do.
>
>JOHN. Trouble is - I got a bit excited and went nearly three times over our limit. (biting a nail) (FAINT LAUGH)
>
>MANAGER. I know. I know. Houses eh ? Houses... But you've got to be comfortable haven't you ? (relaxing back again in his chair) I mean what's the point in settling for some concrete yarded dump, that needs re-stumping, is built next door to a railway line and looks like it's been lived in by vandals?
>
>JOHN. Yeah. (swallows hard, that pretty much describes it)
>
>MANAGER. What's the total damage ?

JOHN takes a deep breath.

>JOHN. We need to borrow about 95... (swallowing quickly) 112 thousand dollars.
>
>MANAGER. No problem, son, no problem at all. I think I can go into bat for you on this one. Why not stick your neck out eh ? (slipping on a stethoscope coming round to John's side of the desk)

> You're young, John, young. What you've got up your sleeve, son, is the most precious commodity of all. (quickly pokes the stethoscope through John's shirt) Time, son. Time. Deep breath in ...

JOHN looks kind of shocked but it all happens so quickly, before he can even protest. He jumps a bit at the cold press of the metal.

> JOHN. Ow.

> MANAGER. Hold it. Breath in.

> JOHN. Sorry - just a bit cold. (breathes in).

> MANAGER. Time, energy, enthusiasm. I'll put my money on those things any day, son.

> JOHN. (feeling a big chirpier) Except Bank Holidays ?

The MANAGER takes JOHN's pulse, holding his wrist, looking at his watch. Ignoring his pathetic attempt at humour.

> MANAGER. Any congenital problems in the family, son ?

> JOHN. No, they're all pretty healthy, thank god. (slight pause). Well, they're all dead, but they *were* healthy when, you know, while they (lived)...

> MANAGER. (cutting him off with a biro on the tongue) Say "Aaar"

> JOHN. "Arrrth"

> MANAGER. You never can say it properly with a great bloody thing whacked in your gob, can you ? (rubbing his hand up and down

JOHN's spine) Still, you've got a good strong back, though, that's the main thing.

JOHN (pulling away slightly - that's going a bit too far) Yes, I do get it massaged regularly.

The MANAGER pats him affectionately on the shoulder.

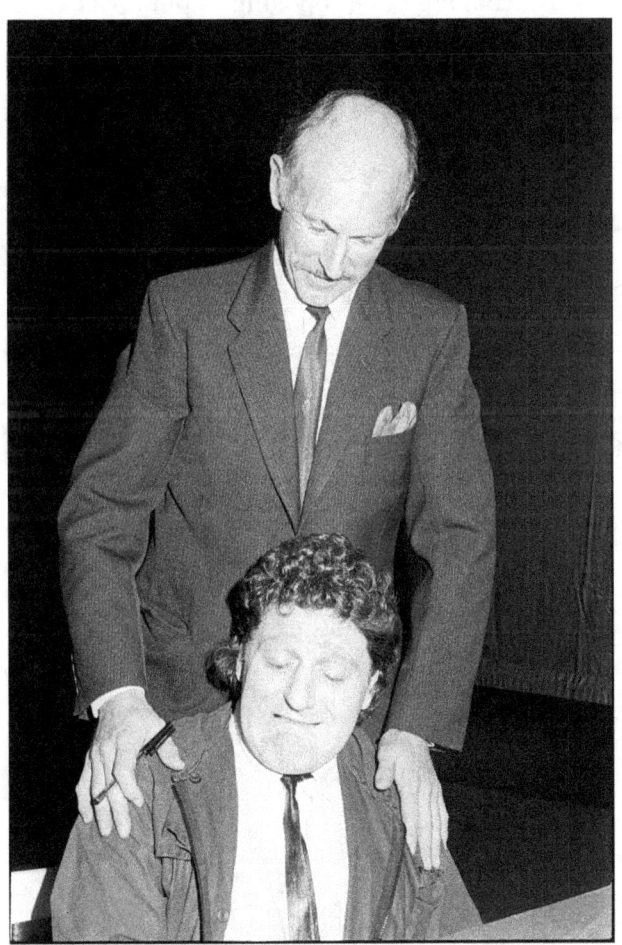

MANAGER. Well, I'm pleased to report you've got a few ye fighting weight left in you yet. You lucky young colt.

JOHN Well, actually, sir, I *am* 38.

The MANAGER looks surprised, and resumes his comfortable chair shuffling some papers, clearly this is older than he expected.

> MANAGER. Oh, well, I suppose we can always reschedule… further down the track… It's not called a *mort*gage for nothing… So - what are you proposing to put up as collateral, John ?
>
> JOHN. (brightly)Well I've got a scooter. (proudly) 40 cc

The MANAGER writes that down.

> JOHN. But I was hoping to use that for the deposit.

The MANAGER crosses that out.

> MANAGER. Liquid assets ?
>
> JOHN. Not much.
>
> MANAGER. Round figures?
>
> JOHN. Oh…thirty or forty…
>
> MANAGER. Thousand?
>
> JOHN. No, dollars…
>
> MANAGER. (writing it down) … thousand dollars.
>
> JOHN. No, round figures…
>
> MANAGER. (trying to comprehend) Yes ?
>
> JOHN. 30 or 40 dollars total … roughly.

MANAGER. Oh I see.

The MANAGER Puts his biro down slowly, sighs. Pinches the bridge of his nose, head down for a moment. Calculating.

MANAGER. Well, I appreciate your honesty, John ... Most people try to lie about their liquid assets. (taps his fingers on the desk) Still, it's earning interest - so let's call it 800 all up.

JOHN. You see, sir, ah ... Sooz and I thought we might share the title - you know combine our incomes, that sort of thing.

MANAGER. Ah - you're Suzi Wiseman's boyfriend?

JOHN. Yeah.

MANAGER. Right, right. Oh, that makes *all* the difference. But let's keep the little woman out of it eh ? (looking around, just to make sure no one's listening)

JOHN. Excuse me ?

MANAGER. Out of the formal side of it.

JOHN. (frowns) I don't ... quite understand.

MANAGER. Look, before you know it, she's off having kids, bored at home, looking for other lovers, hitting the bottle and then where will you be ?

JOHN. (clearly never thought about it) Oh I...

MANAGER. Getting sued for half your property, son.

JOHN. Oh - she'll be awfully disappointed.

MANAGER. Women are *born* to be disappointed, John. That's what keeps them alive! They're so good at it. Their existence'd be truly miserable if they didn't have us blokes around constantly letting them down.

JOHN. (shrugs) I suppose (not wanting to contradict him).

MANAGER. So what's the verdict?

JOHN. Well, I suppose I could go for a bit of overtime at work…

MANAGER. That's the spirit, lad - ah just sign where the cross is, and I'll fill in your Ozcard details later.

JOHN signs and the MANAGER whips the contract away.

5. INT. JOHN AND SUZI'S HOUSE   NIGHT (1987)
JOHN, SUZI

Through the BLACKOUT we hear the sounds of GIGGLING. Bodies THUMPING about.

SUZI. (voice over) Come on, are you a. man or a mouse?

JOHN. (voice over) I'm a mouse. (pause) But you're an elephant.

SUZI roars with LAUGHTER, she snaps the light on beside the door and we see that she's being carried into the room over JOHN'S shoulder, in a kind of fireman's-lift-parody of the bride getting carried over the threshold. Her head almost dragging along the ground at the back of his legs. JOHN'S knees buckle, her weight defeats him, and GIGGLING, they collapse into a single mattress on the floor. For a few moments they just lie on their backs in a bemused, crumpled heap.

> SUZI. (contented sigh) I still can't believe it.
>
> JOHN. Isn't it great ?
>
> SUZI. How about some ... (sensually) mood music.
>
> JOHN. Where's the stereo?
>
> SUZI. I don't know. I asked them to leave it in here somewhere...
>
> JOHN. God there's so much junk.
>
> SUZI. (flinging a few sheets etc. aside) Can't see it ...

SUZI slides into their mattress on the floor. John lies down beside her.

JOHN. Who needs ... music ?

JOHN turns around to retrieve a condom packet from the stuff spread around the floor then slips it between his teeth cheekily tears the wrapper

... and switches the light off.

BLACKOUT.

In the darkness we hear the following in VOICE OVER:

SUZI. (voice over) Oh John.

JOHN. (voice over) Suzi.

SUZI. (voice over) Oh John

JOHN. (voice over) Suzi...

SUZI. (voice over, impatient) Come on -

JOHN. (voice over) Can't seem to... quite get it...

SUZI. (voice over) Oh, John, you're rolling it the wrong way.

JOHN. (voice over) What ?

SUZI. (voice over) Give it to me.

JOHN. (voice over) Hang on.

SNAP OF ELASTIC off.

JOHN. (voice over) Ouch !

SUZI. (voice over) Sorry.

JOHN. (voice over) That hurt.

SUZI (voice over, impatient) You've got it inside out.

JOHN. (voice over, painfully) Ow !

SUZI. (Voice Over) Oh... (pause) It's gone all floppy. Sorry.

JOHN. (voice over, peeved) Well it won't roll on now, that's for sure.

Cheesed off, he rolls off the mattress, gets up and snaps the LIGHT ON, dressed only in y-fronts and a windcheater, he stalks up and down for a few moments.

SUZI. Sorry, John.

JOHN. 'Sorlright.

There's only just a touch of bitterness in his voice

JOHN. It'll come back…probably…

Silence.

JOHN. Eventually.

Silence.

SUZI. We could always tongue wrestle for a bit.

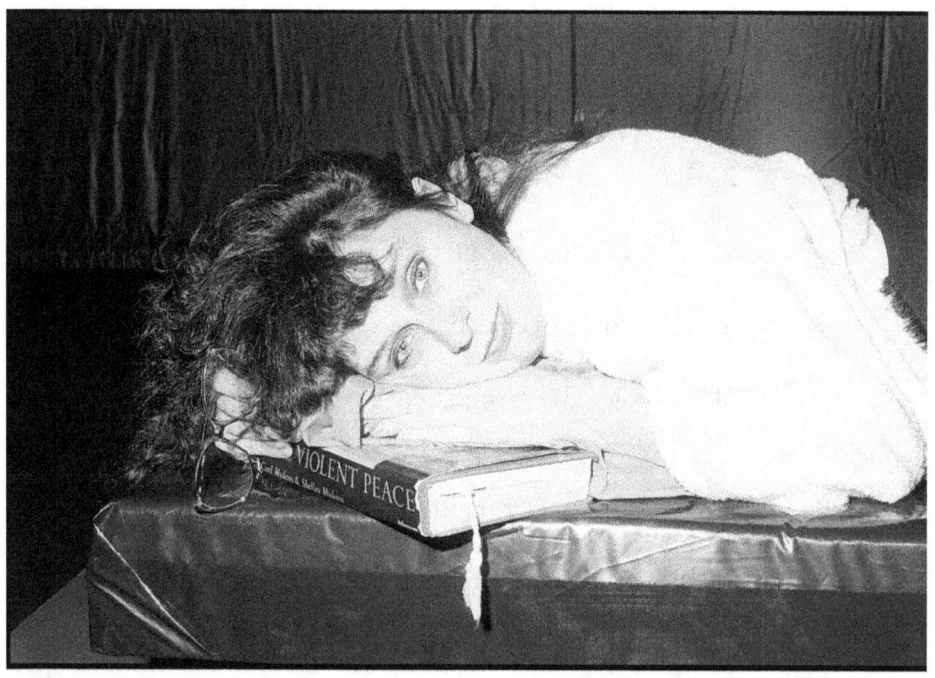

And she lies back down on her copy of "The Violent Peace" looking incredibly seductive.

JOHN is incapable of resisting…

He switches the LIGHTS OFF again.

6. INT. DRINKWATER'S HOUSE   NIGHT (1987)
NORM, DOTTY, SUZI (VOICE OVER)

The LIGHT SNAPS ON in the DRINKWATER'S bedroom.

DOTTY sits bolt up right in bed, her hair in curlers.

> DOTTY. That's the most disgusting suggestion I've ever heard.

NORM is beside her, lying under a copy of the "*Daily Liar*"

> NORM. (chuckles lecherously) Yeah !

> DOTTY. Norm ! Don't just lie there *do* something !

> NORM. Don't think my tongue would reach, Dot.

> DOTTY. Oh ! (unimpressed with him) Can't you ring the police or something ?

> NORM. And say what ?

Next door (still in blackout) SUZI SCREAMS (voice over) in passion.

> DOTTY. It's not natural.

NORM. I dunno, it's how most of us got here;

DOTTY. It sounds like he's strangling her.

NORM. Yeah, some people have all the luck.

DOTTY. I'm not going to put up with it Norm. Not in my own home.

NORM. Well, you never have so far, I can vouch for that.

DOTTY. Don't you care about my beauty sleep ?

NORM. Au contraire, my dear, I've always plumped for
lost causes.

Next door SUZI'S SCREAMS (voice over) peak again.

DOTTY. Oh this is too much !

NORM. (indicating a hole in the adjoining wall) Well, plug up the loud speaker then ! (sticks his head under a pillow)

In exasperation DOTTY frumps out of bed and stuffs a jumper in a hole in their shared wall.

SUZI'S SCREAMS become barely audible.

NORM switches off the light.

BLACKOUT.

7. INT. JOHN AND SUZI'S HOUSE   NIGHT (1987)
JOHN, SUZI, SGT. PRIMUS (Rod Williams) CONST. HANDLING (Jean Kittson)

Meanwhile, next door, still in BLACKOUT the passionate tussle reaches its heady climax:

    SUZI. (voice over) Oh John...

    JOHN. (voice over) Oh Sooze

    SUZI. (voice over) Oh John...

    JOHN. (voice over) Oh Sooze

    SUZI. (voice over) Oh John...

    JOHN. (voice over) Oh Sooze

    SUZI. (voice over) Oh John...

    JOHN. (voice over) Oh Sooze

    SUZI. (voice over) Oh no...

    JOHN. (voice over) Oh yes...

    SUZI. (voice over) Oh no...

    JOHN. (voice over) Oh yes...

    SUZI. (voice over) Oh no...

    JOHN. (voice over) Oh yes...

    SUZI. (voice over) Oh no...

    JOHN. (voice over) Oh yes...Oh yes...

SUZI. (voice over) Oh no…your breath. It's awful

JOHN. (voice over) OH OH OH …

Slight pause. SILENCE.

SUZI. (voice over) Is that it ?

JOHN. (voice over) Huh ?

SUZI. (voice over) 18 seconds flat. That's just about your record, John.

JOHN. (voice over) (feeling pleased with himself) Yeah. Pretty good eh ? (reaching out for her)

SUZI. (voice over) Leave off.

JOHN. (voice over) If only we could feel like this all the time.

SUZI. (voice over) What do you mean "we" ?

JOHN. (voice over) But this is what life's all about - the ordinary moments.

SUZI. (voice over) Yeah, ordinary is right.

JOHN. (voice over) Aren't you glad we came?

SUZI. (voice over) Will you stop using the royal plural.

JOHN. (voice over) No - I mean, St. Kilda. You've got to admit you were wrong about the violence and the crime and all that.

SUZI. (voice over) Well – (shrugs, maybe)

JOHN. (voice over) Go on – it's not as bad as you thought, is it?

SUZI. (voice over) (reluctantly) Well, I suppose...

JOHN. (voice over) I'm so happy. I mean, here we are, we've got a stove, a TV, a washing machine, a stereo, a doona...

SUZI. (voice over) A huge mortgage.

JOHN. (voice over) Almost everything you need.

SUZI. (voice over) Except a Jacuzzi.

JOHN. (voice over) And about three hundred grand in the bank.

They LAUGH.

JOHN. (voice over) Don't move.

SUZI. (voice over) What ?

JOHN. (voice over) I want to get a photo of you.

SUZI. (voice over) Oh, John...

JOHN. (voice over) No - I want to have a memory of us now, at the happiest moment in our lives.

She GIGGLES. He switches the light on, we see he's dressed only in sox, undies, and a sweatshirt reading "Shitter's Ditch First XI"

JOHN. (looking around) Where's the camera

SUZI. (yawning, vaguely) On top of the TV.

JOHN. Which is…? (swinging around, looking)

SUZI. With the video machine.

JOHN. I can't see it.

SUZI. We paid those removalists $400 for two hours work and they leave the place looking like a dog's breakfast.

JOHN (curiously) What's the time?

SUZI. Why?

JOHN. (getting really puzzled) My watch is gone.

She gets out of bed, wrapping a dressing gown around herself.

SUZI. (slow dawning realisation) Oh, my god…

JOHN. What?

SUZI. We've been burgled.

JOHN. Oh no! Ah Christ! Oh Bloody hell

Slight pause.

SUZI. Call the police.

JOHN. We can't.

SUZI. Why not?

JOHN. My plant.

SUZI. Well get rid of it. Flush it down the toilet.

JOHN. Oh, great, thanks a lot. Maybe I'll just smoke it all now.

SUZI. Your solution to everything!

JOHN. I need a joint. I'm tense.

He hunts through his trouser pockets, pulls out a very bent joint

SUZI. And I'll be tense if you have that now.

JOHN. We've got plenty of time to ring the cops.

She shakes her head as he lights up.

Immediately there's a SHARP KNOCK on the door. JOHN and SUZI look at each other, who could that be?

SUZI. (calls out) Who is it ?

HANDLING. (voice off) Police, open up.

JOHN. Shit !

John panics, stamps out smoke with his bare foot, then realizes it *is* his bare foot, and, hopping on one foot, frantically, hopelessly tries to fan the incriminating smoke away.

While the COPS keep HAMMERING away at the door.

SUZI. (trilling pleasantly, buying time) Just a minute…

A second later the whole door crashes down and two PLAIN CLOTHED DETECTIVES storm in.

JOHN is immediately swept up and slammed against the wall by CONSTABLE HANDLING.

HANDLING. Got one, Sarge.

She twists one of JOHN's arms painfully up behind his back. While SERGEANT PRIMUS points a gun directly at his frontal lobe.

PRIMUS. Right, you've got 30 seconds to explain what you're doing here.

JOHN. What *we're* doing here !?

CONST. HANDLING whacks him in the chops, winded, JOHN doubles over.

PRIMUS. Strip him, constable.

JOHN. (still breathless from the blow) Hang on, hang on, I've only got me y-fronts on.

PRIMUS. Taking a few orders, were you son ? What's the Ferret want this week? Videos ? Cameras ? Ladies underwear?

SUZI. (insistent) Look, we live here!

The COPS think that's a huge joke. They LAUGH derisively.

HANDLING. (taking in the bedroom) They've made a right old mess, Sarge.

PRIMUS. Yeah, I've often seen this sort of thing, constable. They don't just rob people who are better off than themselves, they've got to trash their houses, defecate on the floor, its sick!

SUZI. Look! We've only just moved in here! (standing her ground)

Again the COPS LAUGH derisively.

SUZI. (suspicious) How did you know we were burgled? We haven't even rung you yet!

62

That brings THE COPS up short. PRIMUS stops his stop watch, they share an uneasy glance.

> HANDLING. (tentative) There *has* been a burglary here ?
>
> SUZI & JOHN. Yeah. *Us*. *We* were burgled!!

HANDLING lets JOHN go. This requires a slight adjustment of approach.
JOHN pulls himself together as the COPS go into a little huddle.

THE COPS put their heads together, turning away from the young couple, MUTTERING LOW. An inaudible exchange. But they don't look too worried. What have they got to lose ? After a few moments they turn back to SUZI and JOHN. Resuming the suspicious attitude.

> HANDLING. You know it's illegal *not* to
> report a crime, miss.
>
> SUZI. I was just about to pick up the phone
> when you so
> rudely burst in and broke our door!

For the first time the COPS seem genuinely flummoxed. They step back a bit, defensive, cornered. JOHN's confidence returns.

> JOHN. That's right, how come you knew we
> were burgled when we hadn't even called
> you!?

We see DOTTY spying trough the peephole in the fence.

> HANDLING. Oh, I see, I see. Oh yes. When
> the
> copper's late you'd be the first to complain
> wouldn't you ?
>
> PRIMUS. Where's the police they ask, they're
> never around when
> we want 'em. When we call 'em.
>
> SUZI. (almost shouting) We didn't call you !
>
> JOHN. Yet.
>
> PRIMUS. Take this down, constable:

HANDLING makes no attempt to record anything.

> PRIMUS. Name ?

JOHN. John Smith.

PRIMUS. Don't get smart with me, son.

SUZI. It's his name forcrissake ! John A. Smith.

PRIMUS. John a Smith? Are you having a lend of me?

HANDLING. (cutting to the chase) Ozcard ?

JOHN nervously searches his pockets for a moment, finds it, and hands his Ozcard to HANDLING, who shows it to PRIMUS.

Immediately THE COPS relax, put their guns away, close their notebooks and take on a softer, more friendly air - which is almost as unsettling as the aggressive hard-edged, tough cop approach.

PRIMUS.(handing back his Ozcard) At least you've got a few things left, eh John ? (glancing round). So they'll probably be back, you can pretty well count on that.

JOHN. Oh, great.

HANDLING. Joined a video library lately ?

SUZI. Well, yes, as a matter of fact.

PRIMUS. Ah, well, there you go then. Probably heard you giving out your name and address.

HANDLING. Been any house sales around here lately ?

SUZI. This place obviously, I told you - we've just moved in.

> PRIMUS. Ah, well there you go then. Probably cased the joint while it was open for inspection.
>
> HANDLING. 'Course it'll all be sold by now, by the time you got home probably.
>
> JOHN. Sold ?
>
> PRIMUS. Yeah, down at the "Floggers Arms" in Port Melbourne.
>
> HANDLING. Bloke there called the "Ferret", practically holds an auction across the bar. All the latest stolen goods.
>
> SUZI. Well, why aren't you down there arresting him !?
>
> PRIMUS. Sure love, sure, (opening his notebook) Just give us the serial numbers and I'll be down there like a shot.

JOHN and SUZI look at each other, shrug. Shake their heads.

> HANDLING. You have got the serial numbers of the camera and video have you ?

SUZI looks to JOHN.

> JOHN. (sheepishly) Well, actually, no.

PRIMUS snaps his notebook shut. The cops-shake their heads sadly.

> SUZI. What about finger prints?

HANDLING. What about 'em?

SUZI. Aren't you going to take some?

PRIMUS. From where?

SUZI. The window where they broke in.

HANDLING. Too dirty.

SUZI. The door handle?

HANDLING. Too many. (not even bothering to move to check it out)

JOHN. (offering it) My wallet?

PRIMUS. Too messy.

JOHN. (holding it out) A videotape?

PRIMUS. Too dark.

SUZI. The packing cases?

HANDLING. Too difficult. Cardboard's always hard.

SUZI. Look, are you really interested in helping us?

PRIMUS. (putting it the same way) I might put that another way, miss: are *you* interested in helping *us*? As far as I can see you've got no serial numbers, no burglar alarm, no security on your windows, no deadlocks on your doors, you took no reasonable precautions and you practically advertised the fact that you had a video machine all over the neighbourhood.

HANDLING. And - excuse my French - but you took your goddamn time ringing us.

PRIMUS gets up, puts his hat on while HANDLING helps him into his coat.

PRIMUS. And on top of all that you still expect me to tie up extremely scarce police resources with a whole lot of pointless paperwork.

HANDLING. Still, we'll do our best.

SUZI. (sarcastically) Oh Great.

PRIMUS. (as they exit, smiling warmly) Have a nice day.

8. ADJOINING BACKYARDS   DAY (1987)
JOHN, SUZI, DOTTY, NORM

Slides establish the rear of both houses.

DOTTY is vacuuming her backyard. (Yes, with a vacuum cleaner).

JOHN comes out with his dope plant and casts about for a better hiding place. Distracted by the sound of vacuuming he creeps towards the fence and risks a quick glance over the top.

68

He drops down, a bit and stares in hilarious disbelief at the spectacle of someone actually vacuuming a grass lawn.

SUZI comes out with some rubbish for the wheely bin.

> JOHN (whispers) Sooz, check this…
> (motioning her over).

DOTTY'S ears prick up at the sound of JOHN'S voice. She keeps the vacuum running but creeps towards the same spot in the fence as JOHN and SUZI - on the opposite side.

With perfect timing, all heads emerge over the top of the fence at the same moment, in the same spot.

It's an embarrassing shock on both sides. JOHN drops his plant. It slams into his foot. It hurts. He buries any reaction.

DOTTY. (covering quickly, rubbing a finger along the fence top, pointing out the damage) Oh look at that wood rot ! We will have to do something about the fence, you know.

SUZI. (lost for words) Mmm.

Painful smiles all round

JOHN. Nice day.

DOTTY. Good for gardening.

Suddenly paranoid, JOHN reaches out with his injured foot and nudges his dope plant closer to the bottom of the fence out of DOTTY'S line of sight.

DOTTY. I saw the police car last night and I said "Norm, surely we haven't got criminals for neighbours!"

SUZI. Yeah, we were burgled.

DOTTY. Oh dear. Welcome to St. Kilda. (running straight on) Speaking of which - I see you've got the "St. Kilda curse".

SUZI. (slightly affronted) I beg your pardon?

DOTTY. (nodding at the Railway weed, flowing down from the embankment) Terribly hard stuff to get rid of –especially once it takes root. Still, I suppose you can't wait to do the whole place up.

SUZI. Well, actually we rather like its lived-in quality.

JOHN. 'Afraid we're not much chop as renovators.

This is a bit of a shock for DOTTY.

> DOTTY. (slightly curled lip) Oh.
>
> SUZI. Appearances are only skin deep.
>
> DOTTY. So are boils, dear, but. I. wouldn't want, to live with them growing all over me!

Again, polite, suppressed chuckles all round.

> DOTTY. I don't know what poor old Miss Higgins must think of the place now.
>
> SUZI. Miss Higgins?
>
> DOTTY. The former owner dear. Bit of a nut case now I'm afraid. Of course when she became incontinent, they just had to move her into that awful highrise (indicating the block of flats behind the audience)
> I suppose she must often look down into her old back yard - tearfully reflecting on all the memories you've taken from her.

JOHN and SUZI look up at the highrise, aghast at the very thought of the former owner glaring down at them. JOHN takes off his cardigan and drops it over the plant.

> DOTTY. Still I suppose it all adds to the charm of a place. You never think of the generations of people who pass through your house before you, do you? I mean there's only so much you can find out from misdirected mail. (which reminds her) Oh I nearly forgot - you must try some of my garlic...

She steps down and pulls a string of garlic from her vegie patch. JOHN and SUZI shrug at each other at a loss how to get out of this.

As DOTTY comes back up, holding the garlic out.

> SUZI. Well, actually, I'm allergic to…(garlic)

She's cut off by the sudden arrival of NORM, dressed in his usual dressing gown and slippers. He's pushing a trolley full of booze (wine and spirits on top, beer down below).

SUZI SNEEZES.

> NORM. Oh - she's offering you the formal vegetable sacrifice is she? You're lucky, the last lot were a tribe of skinheads with a very bad drummer. All she gave them was a constant hotline to the local cop shop and a endless stream of letters to the Council.

DOTTY smiles, proud of the memory of it.

> NORM. Poor skinny buggers didn't stand a chance. Only lasted three weeks. (extending his

hand) G'day anyway, Norm Drinkwater's the name.

The men shake hands.

> NORM. Ian's my real name, but after breaking the pledge at age 15 I figured "I. Drinkwater" would have been totally misleading. (turning to his drinks trolley, rolling straight on) Got the courage for a swift one, ah...?
>
> JOHN. John. John Smith.
>
> NORM. (pouring scotches - very large ones) Ice and water or just neat?
>
> JOHN. Well, actually, it's a bit early for ... (me)
>
> NORM. Nonsense - this could be the last day of your life. And even if it isn't it's certainly one less from the overall total. And that's one less drinking day as far as I'm concerned (holding glass of scotch out for JOHN, passing it over the fence)
>
> JOHN. No, really I... thanks but...
>
> NORM. (turning back to his trolley) Well, something lighter, perhaps.   A Pimms or a shandy?
>
> JOHN, (chickening out, deflecting to her) Sooz ?,
>
> SUZI. No, really, it's a bit early for me too, thanks.

NORM. (drinking) Bit early! Depends where you measure it from. I've been drinking solidly now since half past one this morning. So for me you might say it's a bit late !

DOTTY. Oh, stop boasting, Norm, you know doctor ordered you to cut back to one a day.

SUZI. One drink?

NORM. One session.

DOTTY. Yeah - which can last for 5 hours.

NORM. (lifting glass) Anyway, kids, welcome to the most frequently burgled street in Melbourne.

JOHN. (bleakly) Cheers.

9. INT. INSURANCE OFFICE   DAY (1987)
FERRET (Rod Williams) JOHN, INSURANCE AGENT (Jean Kittson)

Slides establish the interior of "TAKE A GAMBLE INSURANCE PTY LTD."

Same desk and chairs as the Bank Manager's Office. JOHN is again in the lower chair studying a range of brochures.

74

The INSURANCE AGENT is waiting in the high chair, ready to pounce.

> JOHN. (As if studying a menu in a restaurant) Ah … I think I'll go for the "Home Fortress" Security Policy Al, thanks.
>
> AGENT (eagerly) With the "Cosy As A Castle" Premium Repayment Plan ?
>
> JOHN. Yup.
>
> AGENT. Excellent choice, Mr. Smith, very wise decision. Now I'll just get your Ozcard details, what suburb was it again ?

JOHN hands over his Ozcard. She glances at the address and reacts.

> JOHN. St. Kilda.

She immediately stops writing, lowers her biro with conspicuous gravity.

AGENT. (shaking her head) Ah no – Ah, ha ha no…

JOHN. (puzzled) What?

AGENT (snorts) St. Kilda !

JOHN. Oh no.

She expels a considered breath, goes on shaking head.

AGENT. Oh no, no, no, no.

JOHN. What - you mean I can't get any home insurance because I live in St. Kilda ?

AGENT. Sorry

JOHN. (protesting) But, but - that's commercial apartheid !

AGENT. All insurance is a gamble, Mr. Smith, risk costs money I'm afraid. Your area has three times the number of burglaries as any other suburb. Why your … (checks statistic) street alone, every house in Batman Street's been robbed at least twice in the last 14 months.

JOHN. (collapsing back into chair tragically) Yeah, I know. I know, that's why I'm here. We were cleaned out while making love on Monday night.

AGENT. (total alarm) You've just been burgled !

JOHN nods, bleakly.

> AGENT. (flummoxed) Well, I'm certainly glad you told me that, Mr. Smith ... (shifting papers nervously) 'Course, we, ah, we would have found out anyway. Oooh no. I don't think ... No.

She starts putting the Home Fortress Brochure back in her file.

> JOHN. (almost breaking down) Please, I can't afford to lose anything else. I mean a machine - you can always buy another one - but Christ if they took my tapes, my precious Hollywood collection I'd be devastated.

The FERRET walks in. Stops. Walks out again.

> AGENT. They'll definitely be back you know.

She's holding the file half open again, offering a faint hope. But then closes it again.

> JOHN. (nods sadly, sighs) That's what the cops said.

> AGENT. (she turns, taking out another file) Have you considered one of our 100% fireproof vault units for that priceless Hollywood collection? I can offer a pretty good deal on our new storage facility at Warrandyte…

The phone starts ringing. JOHN takes the brochure.

> JOHN. I'll think about it.

BLACKOUT

EXT. DRINWATER'S BACKYARD   TWILIGHT   (1987)
NORM, DOTTY, JOHN, SUZI, DELIVERY GIRL (Jean Kittson)

FADE UP on:

Coloured party lights decorate the hills hoist in NORM and DOTTY'S backyard. A stunning late summer/early autumn twilight. The SCREAMS of the kids on the nearby "Big Dipper" ride at Luna Park come across in waves.

DOTTY is in the backyard setting four TV Dinner Trays in front of four seats which all face towards an ageing black and white portable TV set. The set is on and tuned to the crassest possible programme that's actually on that night – the reception is terrible. Her hair, as nearly always, is in curlers. We hear NORM'S voice from inside the house

> NORM (off) Dot ? (more impatient) Dotty !

> DOTTY. (trills) I'm in the garden, Norm.

He emerges dressed, as always, in a dressing gown and sox (or slippers) and carries a paper under one arm.

She finishes with the trays and takes up some knitting.

> NORM. Have you seen my copy of the "Daily Liar" ?

DOTTY. (patiently, determined not to be phased by anything this evening, goes on knitting) It's under your arm.

He looks, takes the paper out, holds it, tries to remember why he was looking for it.

DOTTY. (resigned) Oh honestly - *Do* you know why you wanted it ?
(rubbing it in a bit)

NORM. Yeah, I was looking for the TV guide.

DOTTY. I'm using it for place mats.'

> NORM. (just growls at her) Grrrh !

And he starts hunting across the trays for this evening's page. Norm checks the page he's found and changes the channel, but the reception is still terrible. He fiddles with the aerial - which is nothing more than an upside down coat hanger twisted into the outline of a map of Australia.

But his fiddling is fruitless

> NORM. (shaking a fist up at it – behind the audience) Bloody high rise!

He bangs the set, a few times, shakes it, but still no use, and with a muttered curse slams the TV Guide down and settles in his arm chair.

Both NORM and DOTTY are instantly sucked in to what ever is on the box.

After a few moments we hear the OPENING BARS of "*Life Is Great In the Sunshine State.*"

Nothing happens, they remain hypnotised (particularly by the ads, in fact, DOTTY starts channel switching, actually hunting them out between bits of programme - looking for things to buy).

Again the opening bars of "*Life Is Great In The Sunshine State.*"

> DOTTY. Somebody at the door, Norm.

> NORM Mm. (still absorbed by the TV, topping up his glass)

After a few more moments.

>NORM. (making no move) I'll get it.

For a third time the "DOORBELL RINGS out its *"Sunshine State"* tune.

>NORM. Coming.

But it's DOTTY who answers it, still casting glances back at the set.

>DOTTY. Ah - here they are !

JOHN and SUZI stand there, dressed fairly formally - a huge contrast to their hosts. JOHN is holding a bottle in a brown paper bag. NORM goes straight for it.

NORM. You didn't have to bring that.

Opening it with practiced ease, while DOTTY fetches glasses.

JOHN. You might want to let it breathe for a while, Norm, before we kill the bastard, eh ? (chuckles)

NORM sniffs the red wine, regarding the label dubiously, swishes it around his mouth, gargles, swallows, reacts…

NORM Let it breathe ? What - for about 3 years!?

DOTTY. (laughing) Norm !

NORM. I suppose we could always use it for cooking. No - only joking - we'll save it for later when we're so pissed we'll drink anything (puts JOHN's bottle aside) Sherry to start with ? Chardonnay to cleanse the palate ? I'm sure you must be thirsty. My tongue feels like it's just licked the glue off a whole: packet of Tally Hos.

As NORM charges all their glasses.

SUZI. How practical - all you glasses seem to be old honey jars.

NORM sniffs his drink, checks the colour, swishes a gobfull around, savouring it.

Meanwhile DOTTY continues to hunt down her favourite ads as she rides shot-gun on the channel selector.

> NORM. (explaining) Dot has this strange theory: the Networks have conspired to put their ads on all at the same time. Bloody ridiculous. She misses out on entire products now, unless they're repeated on several different channels.
>
> DOTTY. (agreeing) It makes it very hard. In the good old days I could channel-switch virtually all night and not have to watch any programmes at all.

SUZI is pressing her hands to her ears.

> SUZI. Excuse me - I'm sorry, could … could you perhaps switch it off, please?
>
> NORM. What ?

NORM and DOTTY stare at her dumbfounded.

> SUZI. The TV.
>
> DOTTY. (concerned) What's the problem, love ? (turning to him, this could be serious) Turn it down Norm.

NORM lowers the volume. Not switching it off completely.

> JOHN. Sooz goes to Telly Anonymous.
>
> NORM. (still at a loss) Eh ?
>
> SUZI. I'm… I'm trying to give it up.

DOTTY and NORM just stare at her, open mouthed. They cannot for the life of them fathom why.

JOHN. (putting a comforting hand on her knee) Sooz has been doing group encounter sessions now for over 12 months.

DOTTY. (tragically) Oh.

NORM. I'm sorry to hear that, love.

SUZI. No, no, I feel a lot better without it.

DOTTY. (trying to find common ground) Yes, well some of the programmes aren't worth it, are they ? Even my little cocker-spaniel won't watch many of the US soaps these days.

SUZI. (close to cracking) Just that, you know, it's hardest at those special times of the night: 6, 7, 8.30, the late news, when you know… people are doing it all around you.

JOHN. (sympathetically) She was quite a heavy user.

But, unable to help herself, DOTTY has been inevitably distracted by a new set of ads (or whatever)…

DOTTY. (vaguely - concentrating more on the TV than her guests) Sorry, what was that ?

NORM. (aggressively/impatient) She's a sandwich short of a picnic, switch it off!

A bit shocked by NORM'S sudden tone, DOTTY does so. They regard SUZI as if she's got some terrible disease. JOHN shuffles uneasily in his seat, twirling his glass.

DEAD SILENCE.

> SUZI. I just can't seem to eat with the TV on … sorry
>
> NORM. No, no, it's not your fault.
>
> DOTTY. There's no need to apologise, love.

Again DEAD SILENCE, as if without the TV on the key social lubricant of their lives is gone.

NORM and DOTTY stare blankly, perhaps almost wistfully at the blank screen. They try to understand, but can't really comprehend it.

Suddenly the SCREAMS of the kids on the Big Dipper at Luna Park can be heard again.

> NORM. (frowns, curious) What's that sound?

They all listen.

JOHN. That's - I think that's the kids on the Scenic Railway at Luna Park.

DOTTY. Is that what that is?

SUZI. Funny how it comes to you in waves ... (recreating the wave shape in mid air) like the ... like the waves of the Big Dipper itself!

NORM. Never heard it before.

DOTTY. Well, you never switch the TV off, do you?

Again the OPENING BARS of "*Life Is Great In The Sunshine State*" can be heard.

DOTTY. (relieved) That must be Pappalinos.

NORM goes to answer it.

JOHN (brightly) Oh, are there more guests coming?

DOTTY. No, love, it's the take away - hope you like pizza.

Now its JOHN and SUZI'S turn to look incredulous.

NORM goes to open the door and is fumbling with his wallet.

THE DELIVERY GIRL is standing there in a pretty silly uniform.

PIZZA GIRL. Pappalino's Pizza.

NORM. Ah - sorry, mate, I only seem to have a century on me.

He is holding out a $100 note which we notice has holes in it similar to the $100 notes we've seen in the Bank.

JOHN. Ah, here, let me Norm…

JOHN reaches for his wallet.

NORM. Put that away.

JOHN. Don't be silly.

DOTTY. Nonsense, you're our guests.

SUZI. You're providing all the drinks. (second thoughts) Well some of them.

NORM. No, no, I won't hear of it.

JOHN. No no no no no.

DOTTY. No no no no no.

NORM SUZI JOHN DOTTY. (together) No no no no no no no no no

There's a CHORUS OF "NOS" and a kind of progressive tag as everybody tries to put everybody else's money back in some other person's wallet.

There's a pause as everybody collectively realises they've completely lost track of what notes have gone into whose purses or wallets. Only NORM is easily able to identify his holed $100. He takes it back out of SUZI'S wallet.

NORM. I think that's mine.

JOHN. We'd love to pay for it.

So JOHN hands over $30 to the DELIVERY GIRL

JOHN (taking the pizza box from her) Keep
the change.

The DELIVERY GIRL just sort of stands there curling her lip at the three $10 notes JOHN has given her. He's rather pleased to be able to close the door in her face. Checks his wallet. It's empty.

DOTTY takes the pizza off JOHN and starts dividing it into quarters and putting the bits on top of each other in the electric frypan, which she switches on.

NORM (charging his glass) Sorry to hear about your burglary, mate.

JOHN. (philosophical shrug) Yeah (oh well…)

NORM. You're still glad you made the move, I hope?

JOHN. Oh yes.

SUZI. Pity about the trains though.

DOTTY. What trains ?

SUZI. They're closing the St. Kilda rail line down.

DOTTY. (news to her) Are they ?

NORM. And a bloody good thing too.

SUZI. (shocked) What ?

NORM. Half the trains at night are empty love. People are too afraid to travel on 'em.

SUZI. If they spent a fraction of the cost of destroying it on a proper
and more frequent service, more people would use the thing.

NORM. Well the government's gotta cut costs.

SUZI. What's the saving ? If you're going to get from here to the city
in future you better take a thermos and a cut lunch cause the bloody light rail's going on the road system!

JOHN. Sooz, please, let's not have one of your crack-ups darling.

SUZI. Crack ups! Oh I see, this is like Russia now is it? As soon as anybody disagrees with you, you put them in a mental hospital!

But she's SHOUTING and it's not a good look. There's a pause.

NORM is holding what's left of JOHN's bottle of red.

NORM. More grapes of wrath, anyone?

JOHN. Now you're being ludicrous.

SUZI. (stands, gathers her bag) NOW I'm going.

DOTTY. But you haven't had your pizza, love.

JOHN. (reluctantly standing) I think we ah, should push on. . .

NORM. Good.

He goes straight back and switches the TV set on, plonks himself in front of it.

DOTTY. (holding JOHN back) No, please, please don't go.

JOHN. (nodding back at Suzi who waits near the door) Bit of a nervy I'm afraid.

DOTTY. (still restraining him) But I invited you here tonight because… because it's Norm's birthday.

That's a bit of a shock, NORM continues to stare resolutely at the TV set. DOTTY quickly fetches a cake from behind Norm's Esky.

DOTTY. And besides, we won't be able to eat all this by ourselves. (as she moves towards Norm) (sings) Happy birthday to you. Happy birthday to you

JOHN and SUZI tentatively join in the song at DOTTY's encouraging.

DOTTY. JOHN. SUZI. (singing together) Happy birthday dear Normie (Dot says "Daddie") Happy birthday to you...

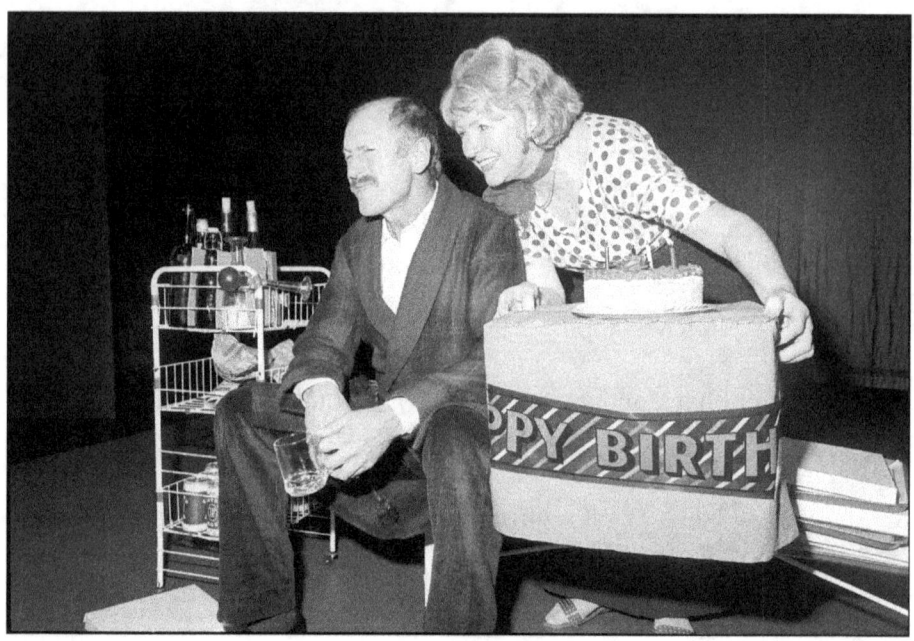

DOTTY places the cake in front of NORM and immediately produces a brightly wrapped present about two foot high. Only this finally manages to distract him from the TV. His eyes light up.

>JOHN. Sorry, Norm, we had no idea. We would've brought something...

>DOTTY. (waving that away) Nonsense.

>JOHN. You should've told us, but...

>NORM. No, no. I've never been one to skite about me age. (holding DOT'S present up, admiring the birthday wrapping paper)

>DOTTY. He's a funny old coot, like that - aren't you love?
>Well, go on, open....

NORM needs no prompting, he eagerly tears at the paper - only to stare open mouthed and aghast at the spectacle of a plump white bird of no definitive plumage inside a wire cage.

>NORM. (aghast) Good, god, Dot.

>DOTTY. (oblivious to NORM'S less than enthusiastic reaction, she coos encouragingly to the bird through the wire) Hullo cockie ! Hullo pretty boy ! Say "Get me outta here" (laughs).

Slight pause, DOTTY continues to make encouraging faces through the wire.

>JOHN. He's very quiet.

>DOTTY. (brightly) He'll find his voice soon enough, won't you cockie?

>NORM. Dot - it's a seagull. Will you stop trying to talk to the bloody thing.

>DOTTY (trying to cover a slight confusion) Norm's footy team. He's the club secretary, you know.

NORM. The Seagulls Board of Directors would shoot me if they heard about something like this.

SUZI. (leaning in, squinting at the cage) It's a pigeon isn't it ? You know, one of those one's you can eat?

NORM. Good, fire up the Barbie, Dot, let's get this over with.

DOTTY. (horrified) Norm ! Don't even joke about it.

JOHN. Looks more like a small albatross to me.

DOTTY. Oh, stop it all of you. It says here (reading the receipt) its a genuine Australian

Bush Galah, with a guaranteed vocabulary of 16 words.

NORM. Well, that's more than Kylie managed at that fancy private school you sent her to.

SUZI. Look, I'm sorry about before …

DOTTY. Don't worry about it love.

SUZI. No- no- I shouldn't have runoff at the mouth like that.

JOHN. At least we've still got free speech, eh ? Not like Queensland.

There's a tense pause.

NORM. (blandly) Dot and I are from Queensland.

JOHN realizes he's put his foot in it.

DOTTY. We came to St. Kilda for a 2 week holiday 30 years ago.

NORM. (quoting) If it's hot in Brisbane its gotta be Cool-in-gatta! (CHUCKLES)

JOHN. (incredulous) You'd swap the Gold Coast for Melbourne ?

NORM. Any time mate, no worries.

SUZI. What about the climate ?

NORM. What about it ?

DOTTY. The humidity up there is shocking.

> NORM. Hot as buggery when it isn't raining, then it's hot as buggery and wet to boot.
>
> SUZI. But it's so *cold* in Melbourne.
>
> NORM. I like the cold. It keeps your brain alive. Besides - what can beat a Melbourne autumn eh ? A beautiful twilight like this, an enchanting sea breeze, not a cloud in the sky…
> (looking up - gesturing expansively)

Suddenly there's an very loud CLAP OF THUNDER, the lights BLACK OUT and come on again. In the next moment its pouring (SOUND OF HEAVY RAIN) and everybody's in a blind panic as they grab things and race inside …

BLACKOUT

11. INT. DRINKWATER'S HOUSE   NIGHT (1987)
NORM, DOTTY, JOHN, SUZI

As they race inside there's a CRASH OF GLASS somewhere off.

> SUZI. (suddenly on alert) What's that?

NORM and DOTTY share an uneasy look.

> DOTTY. Must be the storm

There's more THUMPING and THUDDING OF FEET, which seems to be coming from quite close by.

> JOHN. That's not thunder. That sounds more like ... voices,
>
> DOTTY. (with faint hope, looking at NORM meaningfully) The stereo must be picking up another cab radio, Norm.

That seems highly unlikely. Norm just glares at her with one of those "I told you so" looks.

> SUZI. Cab radio ! Bullshit, that's coming from our place !

She looks up at a painting of the ubiquitous green-faced Chinese Woman on NORM and DOTTY'S wall. Curious, JOHN follows her look, takes the painting down, and is even more confused by the three neat holes drilled in it (though the mouth and eyes of the Woman)

SUZI however, has spotted the three holes behind the painting, she jumps up on a chair and glances quickly through one of them.

> SUZI. (rounding on Norm and Dotty, dumbfounded, accusing) You can see right into our bedroom.

Suddenly an extraordinary ALARM sound goes off.

> NORM. What the hell's that?
>
> JOHN. (handing NORM the painting - tersely) I think that's our Tactical Response Burglar Alarm and Man-trap Package going off. Would you excuse us for a moment. . .

But SUZI is already out the door. With a disappointed look back at both of them. JOHN quickly follows.

NORM. Now, I really need a drink.

12. INT. JOHN AND SUZI'S HOUSE /BACKYARD NIGHT (1987)
JOHN, SUZI, DOTTY.

SUZI races in. Quickly followed by JOHN.

>SUZI. (aghast) They've taken everything…Literally everything.

JOHN switches off the ALARM and then notices an empty box.

>JOHN. My tapes! (slams the box against a wall) Shit !

>SUZI (SCREAMS) Don't do that! Every time you do that something dies in me John. I'm sick of your tantrums, your gaffer tape life-style, your snoring, your clumsiness …

>JOHN. (starts rolling one) I need a smoke.

>SUZI. Your addictions !

She moves to phone. Starts dialing.

>JOHN. What are you doing ?

>SUZI. I'm ringing the police.

He physically stops her. Pushing the disconnect button.

>SUZI. We have to, to claim the insurance.

>JOHN. We haven't got any insurance.

He starts getting undressed for bed. Taking off his trousers

SUZI. What ?

JOHN. It was cancelled.

SUZI. How? (open mouthed) Why?

JOHN. I couldn't afford the premiums. They're astronomical for around here.

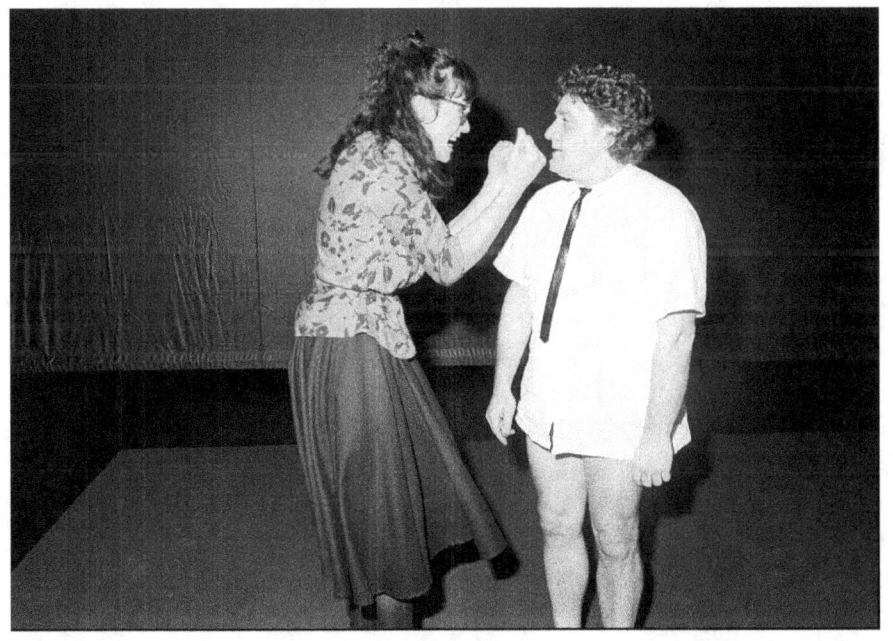

SUZI. Why didn't you ask me for the money

JOHN. (shrugs) I thought with the Burglar Alarm and the
Man Trap we'd be (alright)

SUZI (cutting in) You bloody IDIOT !!

JOHN storms out SLAMMING the door.

13. ADJOINING BACKYARDS   NIGHT (1987)
JOHN, SUZI, INSPECTOR RAMSHOTTT (Jean Kittson),
SGT. JACK BOLT (Rod Williams) DOTTY, NORM

But as soon as JOHN comes out he realises he hasn't got a match for his smoke, he pats his windcheater, turns to open the back door, but, of course, it's deadlocked. He shakes it.

> JOHN. (flinging joint, away) Shit !

Next door, checking that the coast is clear, DOTTY sneaks out with a basketful of clean washing and proceeds to hang it up - using this as a cover to go on spying.

A moment later JOHN and SUZI's front DOORBELL RINGS.

We hear SUZI'S strangely pleasant voice off.

> SUZI (off) (trills-warning) John, dear, the police are here !

John goes into absolute panic, he scrambles to find the joint he's just thrown away, slips it behind his ear, grabs his "plant" and frantically races about looking for a place to stash it.

He is about to slip it round the corner into NORM and DOTTY'S backyard - only to find her hanging up the washing. So he instantly retreats back behind his wheely bin, crouching out of sight of the back door.

> SUZI. (off) John, dear, Inspector RAMSHOTT would like
> a word... (she checks-around the yard disappears inside again)

While JOHN catches his breath behind the wheely bin we hear the BELLS of the level crossing and the FLASHING RED LIGHT announce the imminent passing of another train. JOHN looks aghast in both directions up and down the railway line,

He goes to hide from the train on the house side of bin, just as SUZI'S head briefly pokes out around the back door again.

       SUZI. Are you out there, dear?

Trapped between the train on one side, and the police on the other, JOHN has no other place to go, he quickly rips the plant out of the pot in order to stuff it under his windcheater ...

... and dives head first into the bin - just as the train ROARS past.

SUZI, tentatively, ushers INSPECTOR RAMSHOTTT out into the yard. RAMSHOTTT. (She looks exactly the same as CONST. HANDLING in the earlier scene.)

Next door, DOTTY has run out of washing to hang up and quickly goes to fetch another load so she can keep eavesdropping.

>RAMSHOTT. (opening a clipboard) Now, let me see… 27 Batman Street…ah yes, we've come about the burglary.

>SUZI. (open mouthed) But we haven't even rung you yet.

RAMSHOTT double takes.

>SUZI. That's what I've just been saying. John and I had a huge fight about it. He didn't even seem to think it was *worth* ringing you.

>RAMSHOTT. Ah - men. They're all the bloody same aren't they? Pigheaded, hopeless and pathetic at the best of times.

SUZI can but only agree.

> SUZI. Yeah. ,
>
> RAMSHOTT. I don't know why we bother putting up with 'em sometimes.
>
> SUZI. Yeah.
>
> RAMSHOTT. It's utterly impossible to engage them in any kind of emotional life. They're incapable of it.
>
> SUZI. I quite agree. John's response to any issue remotely connected with feelings is just to walk away from it. (Still nervously casting about for where he might have walked away to)
>
> RAMSHOTT. (putting a sisterly arm around her) So he bolted off in a huff, has he ? - over this "ringing the cops" business.

SUZI nods.

> SUZI. I hate this part of it … the terrible silence that can go on for days. The oppressive avoiding of eye contact, the hateful sharp gestures and the monosyllabic requests to pass the milk or the addicterine at breakfast - all until *I* apologise and things sort of return to normal … until the next time.
>
> RAMSHOTT. (hugging her close, supportive) Bastard.

But inside the bin John can no longer contain himself.

> JOHN. (popping up out of the wheely bin like a jack-in-the-box) *I'm* the one who always apologises!

The TWO WOMEN reel back. JOHN suddenly realises he's exposing the plant below him and instantly drops down again, his nose level with the edge of the bin.

SUZI and RAMSHOTT fan the smell of the bin away.

> JOHN (dropping the aggression) And I wasn't running away from it.

Recovering, RAMSHOTT advances on the bin, JOHN's beginning to regret his interjection.

> JOHN. (smiling weakly) Hullo, officer, nice evening.

RAMSHOTT accidently kicks the empty pot that JOHN has dropped Prior to scrambling into the bin with his plant. JOHN and SUZI share a despairing glance.

> RAMSHOTT. (examining the pot closely, sniffing it, suspicious)
> Perhaps we could get back to the items you claim to be missing.
> (checks notebook) For example: one National video recorder, model NV 100.
>
> SUZI. That's the old model.
>
> RAMSHOTT. What ?
>
> JOHN. You're talking about 2 burglaries ago, mate. We went through all this last time.

RAMSHOTT looks from one to the other.

RAMSHOTT. You mean to say - other police have already investigated this matter?

JOHN. Can't you people get your act together ?

RAMSHOTT. Plain clothes police?

JOHN. Yes, and they were extremely unhelpful - to put it mildly.

RAMSHOTT lowers herself to his eyelevel coming right up close to the bin - John retreats a bit, but realizes he's more or less stuck)

RAMSHOTT. Perhaps you'd hazard a brief description of these alleged police officers, sir? (biro poised to write)

JOHN. Well, one was a woman, about 5'6", brown hair...brown eyes...

As he continues to describe the previous officer to RAMSHOTT, JOHN slows as he realizes:

JOHN. ...and looked very much ... well pretty much like you actually.

RAMSHOTT. (noting it down, but not reacting) And the other ?

At which point SGT. BOLT (also plainclothed) comes into the yard from inside JOHN and SUZI'S house. He carries a dusting brush and camera.

BOLT. I got a good set of prints off the window...

JOHN (open mouthed) ... looked exactly like him. Only *he* seemed to be in charge last time, and now...

RAMSHOTT. (to BOLT) Take them down to forensic, Jack.

JOHN. ... *you're* in charge.

BOLT disappears.

SUZI. This is incredible.

RAMSHOTT. Not at all, madam, not at all. I'm ashamed to say we are extremely interested in this kind of matter. You see, Sgt. Bolt and I (indicating direction of BOLT'S exit) are from Police Internal Affairs.

SUZI. (relieved) Thank god I thought we were going out of our minds!

RAMSHOTT. (turning to JOHN, and simultaneously turning over another page in her notebook) So perhaps we could start with some indication of your movements over the last 24 hours, sir ?

JOHN. (boggles) *My* movements ? That's a bit personal, isn't it ?
(unable to contain himself he has popped up again out of the bin – but immediately realises his mistake so pops down again, back to below bin level)

RAMSHOTT. (patiently) I only want to get to the bottom of it.

JOHN. Well - they're pretty regular, thanks, how are your
movements ?

SUZI. (warning) John !

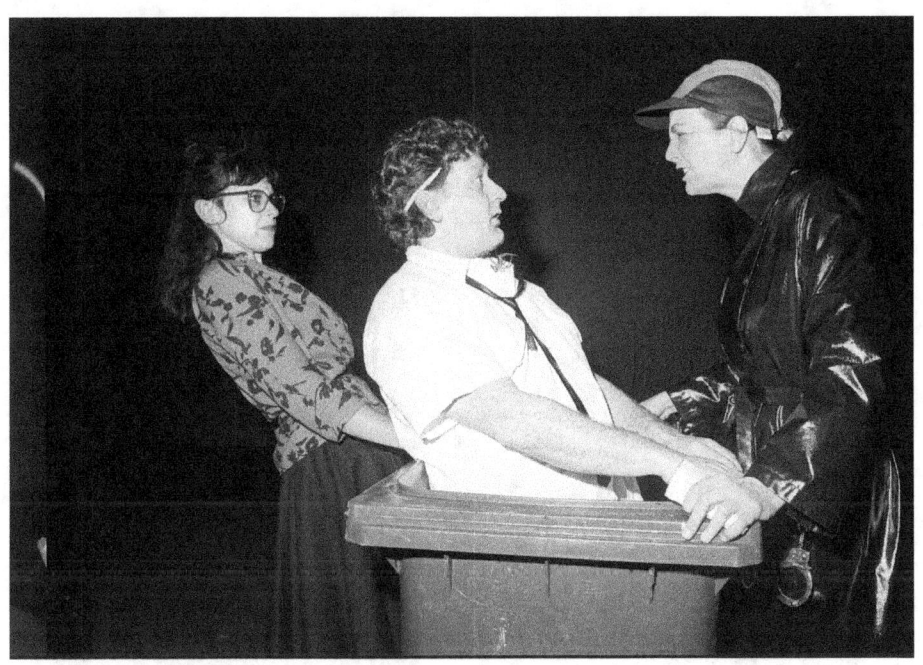

RAMSHOTT. Look, I may seem to be just-another dumb pig to you, John. But us coppers are normal people too, you know. We have normal sized mortgages and normal families that we take on normal holidays to normal places with normal aspirations and I must say it seems pretty damn *peculiar* to me that here I am having a *normal*
conversation with you standing in a wheely bin!

JOHN swallows, trapped. Point taken. Game set and match.

RAMSHOTT moves towards him menacingly.

RAMSHOTT. (striking a cigarette lighter - holding out the flame towards him) Perhaps you'd like a hot connection for that cigarette behind your ear…

JOHN sinks straight back into the bin again, the lid closing over him. RAMSHOTT simply attaches a pair of handcuffs sealing the lid firmly to the body of the bin.

RAMSHOTT (to. SUZI) I'll just take him off your hands for a few more questions (tipping the bin back, preparing to take it away) You can wheel him home again, yourself, when you're ready ...

SUZI. (helping RAMSHOTT to pull the bin away) Oh, don't hurry on my account. I've got plenty of time...

The WOMEN share a laugh and push JOHN off, happily ignoring the desperate, muffled pleas coming from inside the bin

JOHN (muffled) Sooz, Sooz ! Help ! Call a lawyer !

JOHN continues to bang the lid from inside the bin as they roll him off. Straight to the St. Kilda Police station CIB.

INTERVAL

ACT TWO

14. INT.   TRAIN TRAVELLING   DAY (1987)
JOHN, SUZI, NUN (Jean Kittson) PASSNGERS (Rod Williams) (Helen Tripp)

As the stage lights come up we see an extremely disgruntled JOHN, huddling inside one of SUZI'S coats, his bare legs poking through a green garbag, the top of which he nervously clutches around his waist (like a giant plastic nappie).

Oblivious to his discomfort, SUZI, opposite, is scribbling in her notebook.

>	JOHN. (stabbing an accusing glance at her)
>	You could've brought me some clothes.

>	SUZI. You're lucky to be coming home at all.

>	JOHN. Hoh ! A thousand dollar fine ! That's lucky?

>	SUZI. I'd have thrown the key away.

>	JOHN. It'll have to come off your bankcard you know. I've got no money left. (Slight pause) If only I'd remembered the bloody joint behind my ear …

SUZI. (without looking up from her writing) That's what I keep telling you - your short term memory is stuffed. Too much dope.

JOHN. In our society a short term memory is a positive advantage. Besides, as your short term memory gets worse, your long term memory gets better.

She ignores him.

JOHN looks around, picks up an abandoned copy of "The Daily Liar" on the seat beside him. Glances at it.

JOHN (reading paper) Hoh ! I says here only 20% of Americans are
really happy … did you know that ? (no response, he reads on)
I see where there's only going to be three festival-free days next year - between the Homeless Sailor's Week and the Picolo, Post Bicentennial Balloon Twisting Fete.

He glances around the paper at her, waits.

SUZI. Look - this is the last train to St. Kilda, right ? I'm afraid I'm a little busy with the issue at the moment.

JOHN. Last train ? (looks out the window) This, can't be the last train.

SUZI. That's why I'm trying to write this letter, do you mind.

JOHN. But this is the oldest railway line in Australia - I mean, where's the bunting, where's the brass band ? This is an historic moment.

SUZI. It was an historic moment when they closed the *Southern Aurora,* and *The Spirit of Progress* too. But there was no brass band then, either.

JOHN. That's outrageous!

The train stops and NUN gets on. There's no seats left so JOHN stands to let her have his. She looks askance at his strange clothing but sits nevertheless and focuses on her prayer book.

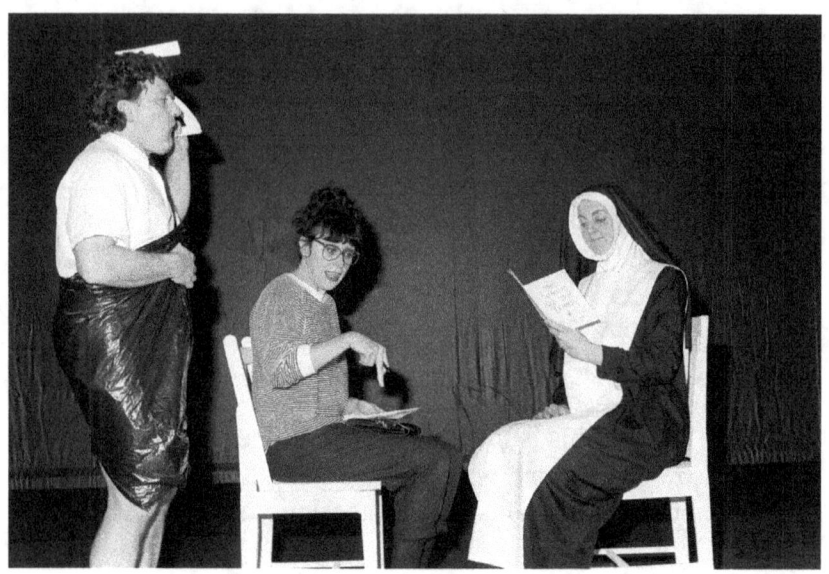

SUZI. There's a meeting in the South Melbourne Town Hall tonight if you really want to do something about it.

JOHN Oh - well, ah, actually, I said I'd go to the Neighbourhood Watch Meeting tonight.

SUZI. I see - off to your vigilante squad, eh ?

JOHN. Ah look – Neighbourhood Watch is about people getting together, talking to each other. Taking an interest. It's about community.

SUZI. If they're so concerned about protecting the community why isn't Neighbourhood Watch out there saving this railway line?

JOHN. It isn't that sort of organisation.

SUZI. Exactly, my point exactly.

JOHN. God you're cynical.

SUZI. Australians are afraid of politics, because they're
afraid of rocking the boat, of getting involved,
of taking a stand,

JOHN. Oh yes, and so what happens if you *do*
save the train line - if you *did* get everything
you wanted, life would have no meaning would
it, for you, without some goddamn struggle ?

SUZI. That's just where you're wrong, John, if
we got everything we struggled for life would
just begin,

JOHN. Well, I don't think you're going to
change the world through the letters to the
editor column of "The Daily Liar".

BLACKOUT on the NUN's reaction.

15. EXT/INT. BACKYARDS/ JOHN & SUZI HOUSE EVENING
(1987) NORM, DOTTY, SUZI, JOHN

Somewhere off SUZI is practicing her Sax - a reprise of the big-city bluesy THEME of the opening scene.

NORM is dressed in his bowls' whites, hat, shoes, clutching a half dozen under one arm and his bowls bag in the other, kicking at his back door with a foot.

NORM (holding the pipe of a breathalyzer) But, Dotty, you've got to let me in. This thing is way out, I tell you. It doesn't apply to someone with my tolerance of alcohol.

DOTTY. (voice off - inside the house) You're not coming in, Norm, not until you can prove to me that you're well under point 05.

NORM. But, look, look, you can check the colour of the crystals yourself if you like.

DOTTY. (off) I can see them from here. They've gone every colour in the rainbow.

NORM jumps to another tack.

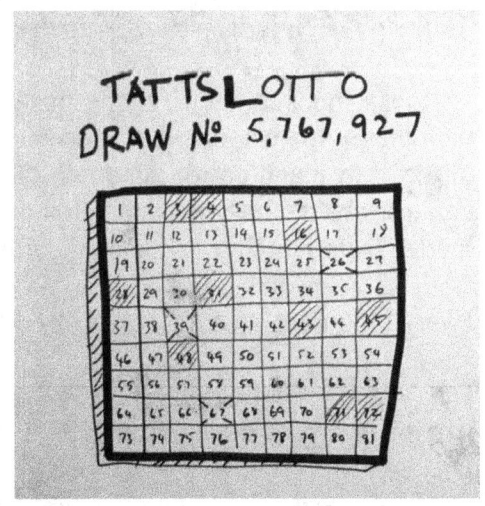

NORM. Telegram from Tattslotto…

DOTTY. (off) What? (momentarily unsure)

NORM. Telegram for Mrs. Drinkwater. Tattslotto Head Office calling.

DOTTY. (off) Oh go away, Norm. You can sleep it off in the park for all I care. I'm sick of it, you hear me?

NORM. (searching about) Alright, if you're not going to let me in I'm going to let Cockie out.

DOTTY. Norm! Don't you dare touch that bird!

No response.

DOTTY. (off) Norm- I'm warning you…

NORM struggles to pick the bird up out of the cage, fumbling around inside it until he manages to grab Cockie and flings it up and out in the air - only to watch it drop straight to the floor.

He looks shocked, then clutches his chest - suddenly there's an enormous pain there - his whole left side seems numb, the carton of cans falls from his other arm and go rolling down the slope of the backyard as he collapses back onto the banana lounge, facing the audience, dead still, but hidden from DOTTY'S line of sight at the back door.

Everything goes QUIET (apart from the SAX).

DOTTY is concerned, but more worried about Cockie than NORM - she tentatively opens the door an inch or two but keeps it on the chain.

DOTTY. (peeking through the gap) Norm…

But from behind she can only see his feet dangling over the side of the banana lounge.

DOTTY. (more sharply) Norm ! (waits) I know you're
playing fox… I think it's pretty stupid in a man
your age. I've got no patience at all for your
silly games. You don't care about me, Norm.
You don't even know what I do all day. You
wouldn't have a clue! You're always down at
your bowls club or the RSL. (pause) You know
what I did today? I'll tell you what I did - I
washed up the breakfast things then I stared at
the wall for about half an hour. At eleven am I
made a cup of coffee. I had a chat with Sheila
on the phone and then I watched -*Midday* With
Ray Martin. There were hardly any ads so I
switched over to *Days of Our Lives* and
General Hospital. After lunch I folded tea
towels for a while and had another cup of
coffee. About three thirty I took the washing
off the line …

It's still very QUIET out there, so she risks slipping the safety chain off and pokes her head through the door.

DOTTY. Norm ? Have you gone to sleep ?

Then she spots the bird lying on the ground, and is immediately furious.

DOTTY. Oh Norm ! What have you done to
Cockie !

She rapidly exits the house and as she pushes past the banana lounge to pick up the bird she throws a quick sideways glance and NORM and SCREAMS.

DOTTY. NORM !!!

The SAX STOPS, the light comes on in JOHN and SUZI'S house. JOHN sits bolt upright in bed - dropping the pillow he's been using to keep the noise of SUZI'S sax out.

Next door, DOTTY is frozen, hands clutching her mouth, fearing the worst. JOHN and SUZI race out into the backyard and virtually leap over the fence. SUZI pulls open NORM'S shirt while JOHN levels out the banana lounge so SUZI can immediately go to work pumping his chest. JOHN takes his pulse, DOTTY remains frozen.

SUZI tries mouth to mouth.

Suddenly NORM'S legs kick out and he seems to shudder back into life…

>NORM. Who's been eating garlic ?

>DOTTY. Oh Norm ! You're alive ! Oh, thank god !

SUZI continues blowing into his mouth.

> NORM. (blinking, shaking his head, can't believe it) I just dreamt I was sleeping with a beautiful fairy princess.
>
> DOTTY. (clearing her throat) I think that's enough mouth to mouth thank you dear. .

SUZI stops.

> NORM. (still vagued-out) Where am I ?
>
> DOTTY. (holding his hand) You're home, Norm, it's alright, pet,
> you're home ... (kissing it)
>
> NORM. (looking around, disappointed, sitting up) Oh gawd !sitting up) What an awful place to cark it ...

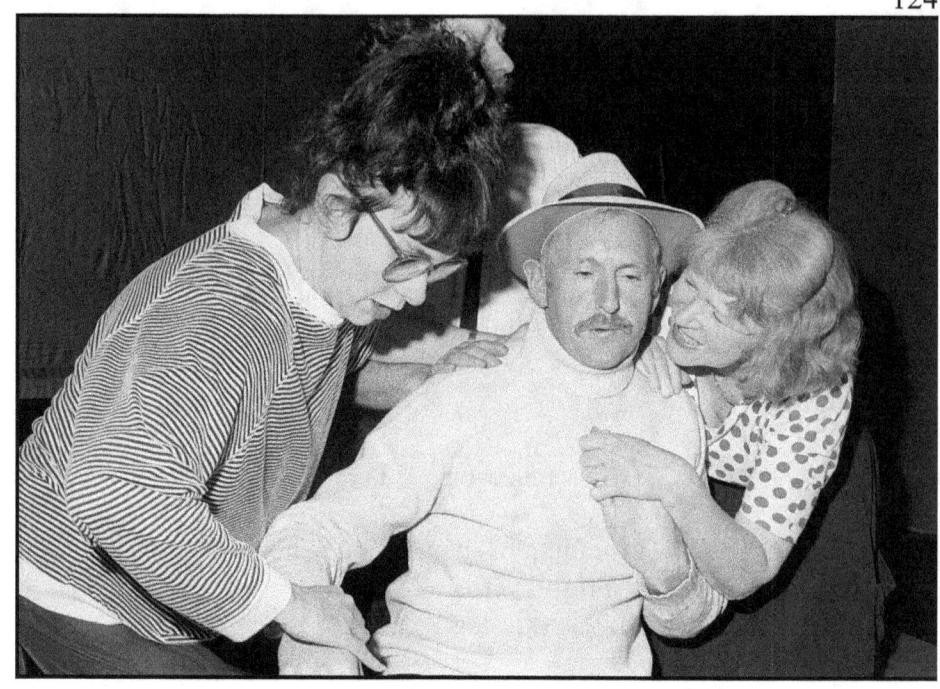

DOTTY (patting his hand) That's just a lot of abalone - you're not going to cark it…

JOHN. Too right, mate, you've just got a bit of a shock that's all.

NORM. It's all that bird's fault. I thought he'd been off his crackers.

SUZI (checking his pulse again) We've got to get him up on his feet, keep him moving, keep the pulse rate up.

DOTTY. I'll ring an ambulance. .

DOTTY rushes inside, while JOHN and SUZI, with some difficulty, heave NORM up onto this feet.

For the rest of the scene the three of them walk a strange dance that defines an erratic path round and round the backyard - with NORM'S legs constantly wobbly, constantly in danger of sinking the whole trio.

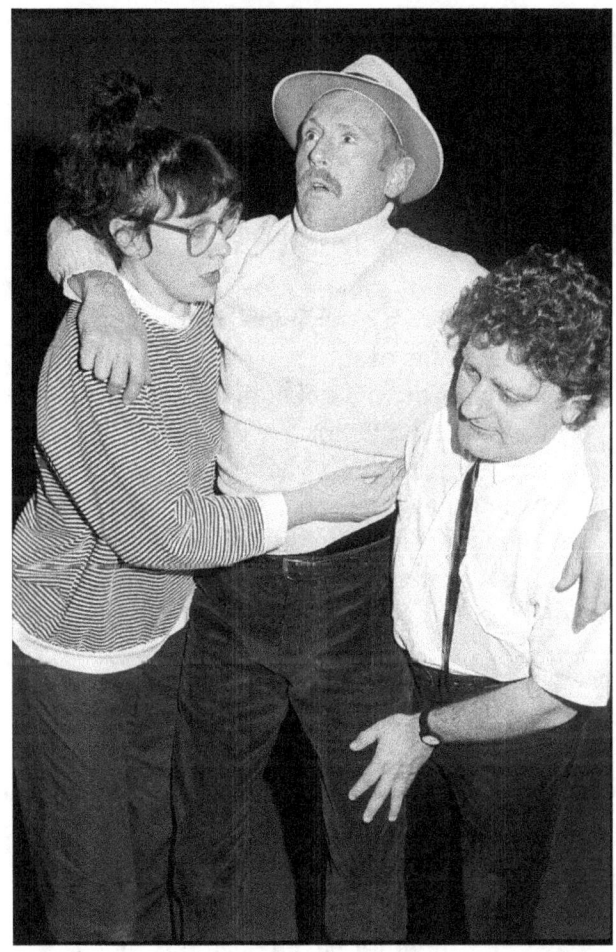

NORM. You're bloody beautiful, you two, you know that?

They laugh.

NORM. No, no, I mean it. You're beautiful people.

SUZI. Well we don't actually drink at the Red Eagle, Norm.

NORM. You're like a son and daughter to me, you know that ? More than that bitch Kylie…

SUZI. Don't be silly, Norm.

NORM. No - you saved my life, I'll always owe you that.

SUZI. It's just basic first aid, that's all. Anybody can do it.

NORM. But not everybody knows how, love. That's the guts of it.
What keeps the old ticker going, eh? Some life force you reckon? Some will to live? As if the spirit's got to want to - before the heart beats anyway. I hate that sadness people get when they feel they're going to die, and they just sorta get sick and pale and kinda give up. I don't want to go like that. I wanta go out on me feet…

JOHN. Well - we're working on it.

But NORM'S legs crumble a bit at this point arid all three of them stagger into the table and knock the birdcage flying. But JOHN and SUZI manage to recover a bit and keep them all vertical.

NORM. Strewth, I haven't had this much exercise since the Second World War.

The SIREN of an approaching ambulance is heard off.

BLACKOUT.

INT. COLESWORTH'S SUPERMARKET   DAY (1987)
JOHN, COLLEEN (Jean Kittson), BERYL (Helen Tripp), THE FERRET (Rod Williams)

>BERYL. (as she rings her cash register BELL)
>Check 100 please.

She's holding aloft a $100 note with several holes clearly drilled through it. MUZAC floods the background.

Beside BERYL is THE FERRET shifting nervously from foot to foot. He even sometimes ducks down to hide under the counter, until somebody he thinks he recognises has gone past.

>BERYL. Check 100.

BERYL continues to bang away on her BELL as JOHN rushes in, airtex shirt, sensible work pants, name clip.

>JOHN. (as he nervously slips on a bow tie from under the counter) Sorry I'm late Beryl, they're picketing the railway line again and I had to catch tram.

He fumbles with the key to a tin of change, takes the note off BERYL and counts out loud ninety eight dollars in change for THE FERRET (he's only bought a toothbrush).

>BERYL. Boss wants to see you.

>JOHN. (knowing he's going to get a roasting)
>Oh shit.

An enormously relieved FERRET pockets his money, flings the tooth brush aside, drops down and slinks past COLLEEN (who's waiting with a basket of massage oil) As he passes her he hands her some more damaged $100 notes and practically races from the store.

At an equally furious pace JOHN frantically stashes the change tin away, grabs a dymo machine and races to label a box of video tapes and stack them on shelves when he notices, and then double takes, as COLLEEN pushes her trolley up to his cash register.

So JOHN comes back to the counter again.

>JOHN. Beryl, would you ah, clean up a milk spill in lane five please, love ?

>BERYL. Ah - what ? (clearly peeved)

JOHN. (moving to take over the cash register from her) Please, love, would you mind?

BERYL. (reluctantly taking mop and bucket) It's not my job, you know. I hate milk, you can never get the smell out.

He blows a kiss at her.

JOHN. You're a real pet, Beryl.

JOHN immediately turns his attention to COLLEEN who's come up with her trolley of goods - consisting only of about a dozen bottles of Johnson's Baby Oil.

JOHN. (bunging on the charm) Morning, madam, lovely day.

COLLEEN. It's raining.

JOHN. Oh... (face drops) You never get to know those things in here. (counting the bottles into a bag - making light conversation) Goodness, you've got enough Johnson's Baby oil here to start a massage (his smile fades as he says it) parlour...

COLLEEN. (as she hands him $100 note with holes in it) Or a kindergarten.

JOHN. Sorry, madam (correcting himself) er ... lady, my whole float's just gone...

COLLEEN. (sailing on out with her oil) That's alright. Keep the change.

He holds the note and follows her exit sort of stunned. Only BERYL coming back snaps him out of it.

BERYL. I can't find any milk spill.

17. INT SOUTH MELBOURNE TOWN HALL   NIGHT (1987)
CHAIR (Rod Williams), ESTER HAZY (Helen Tripp), SUZI,
DEMONSTRATOR (Jean Kittson), SPY (Paul Davies)

Slides establish the interior of the South Melbourne Town Hall where a rowdy public meeting of the People's Revolutionary Bayside Transport Committee is in progress. '

There's a lectern stage centre behind which stands the CHAIR for the meeting. He has to raise his voice to be heard above the din

CHAIR. Order, Order ! Ladies and Gentlemen, please - the next speaker tonight is Ms. Ester Hazy, representing the Ministry of Peak Hour Traffic and Inner-Urban Decongestion ...thank you Ms. Hazy -

ESTER HAZY moves to the lectern.

HAZY. Ladies and gentlemen, the simple facts of the matter are that the St. Kilda/Port Melbourne railway lines were losing money.

DEMONSTRATOR. Rubbish.

HAZY. The Government simply has to economize.

SUZI. You can save 40 million right now, by not going ahead with it.

HAZY. Last financial year the Ministry of Peak Hour Traffic suffered a deficit of one billion dollars - that is the cost of public transport to this community and I put it to you that it is a burden tax payers can no longer bear.

SUZI. What about the costs of cars ? The costs of freeways ? The brain damage from the lead pollution, the 14,000 people killed on the roads since this government came to power ? Does anybody add those costs up when you talk about the costs of private transport ?

SHOUTS of agreement from the CROWD.

CHAIR. Order please -

HAZY. People seem to prefer cars. We can't force them onto trains you know.

SUZI. You don't even try - you let the lines run down so people aren't attracted to public transport and then' you say, "see I told you so, we'd better rip it up."

HAZY. But we're providing an alternative, we're providing the Light Rail ...

SUZI. Yes, and where are the Light Rail systems the Government promised to build years ago - to the great planning disasters of the Eastern suburbs - to Monash, and VFL park and Springvale - where it's needed ?

More UPROAR, CHEERING breaks out STAMPING of feet.

CHAIR. Order, order !

The DEMONSTRATOR passes around a yellow bucket collecting money for the fighting fund, while a SPY (JOHN heavily disguised in pork pie hat and raincoat) comes in and starts blatantly photographing people.

> HAZY. Governments have to respond to ever changing economic circumstances. It can't be straight-jacketed in its response by a set of immutable preconditions...

> SUZI. Well, I say it's time the government stopped lying about figures, and admitted that the real reason for the destruction of the Port Melbourne/St. Kilda railway is capital D Development, for capital P profits, resulting in capital C Chaos when the road system becomes so choked it'll be quicker to walk anywhere than drive a car !

A resounding THUNDER OF CHEERS breaks out, with the CHAIR desperate to be heard through the din.

CHAIR. Order ! Order ! Order !

SUZI. The people who run this state are the same tired, corrupt old bureaucrats who've always run it no matter who's elected.

HAZY. Now, who's talking rubbish

CHAIR. Order!

SUZI This struggle is not only about the saving of a railway line it's also about the people's rights to determine their own future and not have it decided for them in the boardrooms of Collins Street, or New York or London or Tokyo !

Again, the STORM OF SHEERING AND APPLAUSE.

18. INT. LAUNDROMAT   (DAY 1987)
JOHN, COLLEEN, SUZI

The SIREN of an ambulance continues over and transforms into the SOUNDS of a Laundromat interior: washing machines, dryers etc…

JOHN is staring through the venetian blinds of the laundromat out into the street.

We hear his interior monologue as a voice over. This could be done on tape or "live" by the actor playing NORM (off) and COLEEN'S voice by the actor playing SUZI (off).

JOHN (voice over) Another cop car in Grey street. Pros cruising past with arms like pincushions, flogging five minutes of ecstasy for half a cap. The hollow walk, defeated eyes and skinny broken stockings of an army of the night …

He opens a garbag and starts sorting his laundry.

JOHN (voice over) … with about the same life expectancy as my nylon undies in that overheated dryer. (glances through window again) But then, who am I to talk eh? Just another assistant junior sub-manager window shopping on life's highway…

He breaks off the reverie and reacts as he recognises someone in the street.

> JOHN (voice over) There she is again ! Oh god ! Pulling up in a Mercedes. What's she doing coming to a laundromat? Looks like she'd own half a dozen washing machines.

COLLEEN enters from the street and goes over with a key and bank bag to unlock the coin boxes of the vending machines. A little shy, JOHN turns back to sorting out his washing.

Now we hear COLLEEN's interior monologue

> COLLEEN (voice over) Who is this bloke ? Where have I seen him before ? Why is he staring at me ?

She risks a glance, their eyes meet, and John starts putting washing in a machine.

> COLLEEN (voice over) God is he following me ? (panic) I'm being set up!

COLLEEN unlocks a cash tin and quickly empties the coins into a bank bag and then locks it inside an expensive leather briefcase (which we saw her with in the bank earlier).

> JOHN. (voice over) I might have known - she obviously owns the place.

JOHN summons up his courage and speaks out in his normal voice.

> JOHN. Excuse me. (tentative) Haven't I ... haven't I seen you before somewhere ?

COLLEEN starts, clutches the briefcase self consciously, protectively.

COLLEEN. (voice over) Oh god ! Just smile - keep him talking. (normal voice) What?

JOHN. I'm the bloke at the supermarket - you know, Colesworth's ?

COLLEEN (not recognising him) Oh yes … sorry, I'm running late for
my hairdressers.

JOHN (quickly) You buy your Johnson's Baby Oil there. I always wondered why you kept paying us with $100 bills. (shyly) Should've realized - you own a laundromat, small wonder. We just lost our machine in a burglary. I've certainly not kept track of prices - last time I had to use one of these places it was forty cents a load. Now you practically need an armoured car- just to carry the change.

COLLEEN. (voice over) Ok, so he's going to make it look political,
just smile broadly, keep an eye out for police cars, get ready to scream, keep my hands on the money ...

She smiles nervously, keeps a good distance between them - edging out around the walls, risks a glance at her watch.

JOHN (voice over - flummoxed) God is she afraid of
me? She thinks I'm chatting her up. Well, I am,
I suppose. She's so beautiful, must happen all
the time.

He gazes back out the window, still feeling expansive.

JOHN. Sometimes at dusk, like this, you know
- with the seagulls screeching overhead...

She grips her bag ever more tightly and slowly edges her way towards the front door, as soon as his eyes are off her for longer than five seconds she races for the exit and is gone.

JOHN. (continues, oblivious to her exit) I just
think, Christ, I don't want the day to end. I just
want to ... to ... chase the sun right round the
rim of the world . . .

He gestures towards the sunset through the window, expansive and turns back only to find her gone. He frowns a bit, looks round. Outside we hear a Mercedes with a flat battery trying to START.

JOHN. Hey - hey wait a minute...

He scrambles out the door after COLLEEN, just as SUZI enters from another door carrying groceries.

JOHN. (off) Taxi !

SUZI watches him chase after another woman. Drops her bags. Confused. Shocked.

19. INT. THE FLOGGER'S ARMS   NIGHT (1987)
JOHN, COLLEEN, FERRET (Rod Williams)

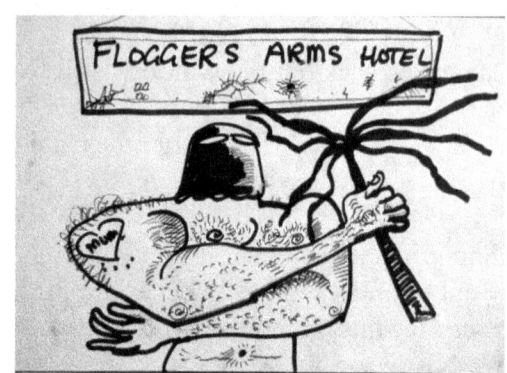

The dim smoky interior of a seedy, run-down pub.

Slides establish this as the "Flogger's Arms" Hotel - the logo consists of two, crossed, black hairy arms holding a cat-o-nine-tails.

COLLEEN hurries in, taking off her fur coat and laundry manager's wig and slipping behind the bar in a black slinky dress that fits in easily with the general bondage theme of the place.

In a dark corner, cowboy hat low over the eyes, with his back to us THE FERRET Drinks, a whip in one hand, a beer in the other.

A few moments after COLLEEN, JOHN rushes in, then pulls up short, his eyes adjusting to the sudden darkness of the place.

Again, MUSIC establishes a bluesy, bit city theme.

>COLLEEN (polishing glasses) Can I help you sir?

JOHN turns to face the bar, not recognising her without the wig etc.

>JOHN. I was looking for someone – thing more formal…

>COLLEEN. What's your poison ?

>JOHN. Sorry ?

>COLLEEN. Drink ?

He comes over, leans in to her, confidential.

>JOHN (meaningfully) Just a couple of tapes, thanks, preferably Hollywood classics.

She baulks, retreats a bit from his personal space. Goes on polishing glasses

>COLLEEN. This is a pub, mate, not a video library.

>JOHN. Alright, a glass of milk, then.

He double takes as she turns round - something in the way the light catches her profile.

>JOHN. It *is* you !

>COLLEEN. (suspicious) What ?

>JOHN. I have seen you before, haven't I ?

>COLLEEN. Well, I'm here Mondays, are you a Monday drinker ?

>JOHN. No - I mean, just now - in the Laundromat.

>COLLEEN. (realises who he is) Look, I wouldn't try anything in here, mate. I've got protection…

>JOHN. (guessing) From the Ferret ? He a Monday drinker too ?

>COTLEEN. Who's he ?

>JOHN. I believe he … he's got a (meaningfully) home removalists' business.

He takes his milk.

COLLEEN. What are you a cop or something ?

JOHN. No. But 1 am interested in a reasonably priced video tape recorder and a set of good quality tapes. Hollywood classics.

COLLEEN. Good quality ! Reasonably priced ? You people, you expect the earth don't you.

JOHN. What ? (thrown)

COLLEEN. Why can't you leave him alone.

JOHN. I've got cash.

COLLEEN. Oh, yes, everybody's got cash, and everybody expects a discount. I suppose you think the Ferret's a soft touch, eh ?

JOHN. (shrugs) I don't know.

COLLEEN. He's always putting his hand in his pocket for blokes like you - with some hard luck story cause you kid's got tuberculosis, or you've just lost your job. The Ferret'll look after it, Ferret always does, good old Ferret.

JOHN. Look, I just...

COLLEEN. Well, I'm sick of seeing him used like this. It's not fair.

JOHN. You, you misunderstand.

COLLEEN. Oh, no, I don't think so. I think I understand perfectly

JOHN. Look, I'm sorry I bloody asked.

COLLEEN. And I'm sorry, but I've got to finish up now. We're closed.

JOHN. Look - (restraining her from closing the bar, holding her arm, she looks down at his hand) I came here because I lost something. Something I value. Very much. And in a strange way I think I've found something - something I didn't expect. .

COLLEEN. (disengaging) Oh - and what's that exactly ?

JOHN. Loyalty, devotion, your concern for this other man, honour among thieves.'

COLLEEN. I've got a slightly queasy feeling you're chatting me up.

JOHN. Is it against the law to tell someone you admire them ? Are we so suspicious of strangers now that we can't take people at face value anymore ?

She holds his look for a moment, then quickly reaches under the bar and puts her coat back on.

COLLEEN. Sorry- I've got a train to catch.

JOHN. They've all been cancelled.

COLLEEN. What ?

JOHN. The St. Kilda line - it's closed.

COLLEEN. Oh, no, that's where you're wrong. There'll always be at-least one train ride left in St. Kilda … and I always catch it after work.

EXT. ESPLANADE ST. KILDA   SUNSET (1987)
JOHN COLLEEN

We hear a VOICE announcing:

> VOICE OVER. Scenic Railway, Scenic Railway, Departing now. Stand clear, please. Stand clear !

CUT TO: Luna Park. A funfair by the sea.

Amid projected images of Luna Park JOHN and COLLEEN stagger into view, laughing and exhausted from the sheer lunacy of it all.

>JOHN. And you do that every day ?

>COLLEEN. Nearly every day.

>JOHN. The last time I rode on the big dipper at Luna Park the woman behind me vomited all over my suede leather jacket.

COLLEEN smiles, looks around, takes in the palm trees.

>COLLEEN. From certain angles you'd think we were in a movie about the foreign legion: silver domes and palm trees and strange forts like Luna Park.

>JOHN. You could be Myrna Loy, and I'd be your sheik in shining armour.

>COLLEEN. (laughs) I think you're getting your genre's a little mixed up.

JOHN. (looks at her meaningfully) Or my feelings …

COLLEEN. (meaningfully back) Well, yes - if you're acting out some
Saturday arvo, matinee-at-the-pictures fantasy.

JOHN. I always used to as a kid… don't see why I should stop now.

COLLEEN. Let's not get too excited.

JOHN. I mean, of the odd half million hours we've go in a normal life span how many of them are truly memorable? Of how many can we honestly say "there", "then" I was truly alive.

COLLEEN. Well, you're asleep for about half of them to start with.

They reach the footbridge over the Lower Esplanade and stop, looking out past the St. Kilda pier to the setting sun on the other side of the bay. She looks at the view. He looks at her.

JOHN. Tell me something straight - am I following you, or are you following me?

COLLEEN. I'm afraid - I've been quite unable to follow most of what you've been saying for some considerable time.

JOHN. Can I see you again? Just to confirm that?

She looks at him.

COLLEEN. You'll have to catch me first.

And LAUGHING, she races off down the spiral ramp of the footbridge.

LAUGHING he chases after her ... miming the dizzying effect of the footbridge's, sharp turnings.

21. INT. COLLEEN'S ROOM   NIGHT (1987)
COLLEEN JOHN

They come into her room, still running. He pulls up short. Takes in the place.

>JOHN. Gosh. Leather mattress - must have cost a bit.

She shrugs.

>JOHN. Don't you have any sheets ?

>COLLEEN. Oh, no- the oil tends to stain them.

>JOHN. Your house looks so spartan, so simple. When we were first burgled we had so much stuff we didn't realise it for half an hour.

>COLLEEN. I prefer to live like this, I like to be able to leave a place at a moment's notice.

>JOHN. Is that a threat - or are you just trying to cheer me up ?

>COLLEEN. I value my privacy, that's all - my freedom to move.

>JOHN. Freedom ? What's that ?

>COLLEEN. What most people are most afraid of - free love, an open mind, a one-way ticket to somewhere else.

>JOHN. Look, I'm all for freedom. God !I watched Woodstock on the original broadcast, I even still have some Lenny Bruce records.

(correcting) Well, had…until you know… the (burglary)

She rubs some oil into her hands as JOHN tentatively unbuttons his shirt, sits on the "bed".

        JOHN. It's just my elbow actually, bit of teno
        from the cash register at work.

She starts rubbing his elbow, massaging the oil in. He relaxes a bit.

        JOHN. Only one pillow?

        COLLEEN. My husband OD'd four years ago.
        I've been more or less a solo act ever since.

        JOHN. I'm sorry to hear that.

        COLLEEN. (philosophically) Ah - his kidneys
        were stuffed anyway.

Your liver's rooted if you drink, your lungs if you smoke, and, it seems, your whole immune system if you have any kind of sex at all.

JOHN. They used to call it the "wages of sin."

COLLEEN. Luckily none of them turned up in my pay packet.

JOHN. I'm glad to hear it.

COLLEEN. Nick - my husband, he copped the lot. The last few years were a living hell. I think he reached a point where he just … gave up.

JOHN. You don't have to talk about it.

COLLEEN. Oh - I want to talk about it. I have to talk about it. It's what I call my "ancient mariner complex".

JOHN. Well, I'm all oars…

COLLEEN. So much of what passes for conversation these day seems to me to be a kind of worn out code. We're always editing out what we really feel.

JOHN. Who are you ? Really ?

COLLEEN. (smiles). You don't seriously expect me to know that do you ?

JOHN. I'm not talking philosophically, I'm just wondering what I call you?

COLLEEN. No names, no pack drill.

JOHN. What ? Like a sort of ... "Lust Tango in St. Kilda"?

She finishes rubbing his arm.

COLLEEN. You can put your shirt back on now. Come and see me again next week. (handing him a card)

JOHN. I can't afford to get involved, you know. It's too complicated.

COLLEEN. Because you're married. .

JOHN. No - We only share a mortgage.

COLLEEN. That's worse.

JOHN. Yes, I know.

She takes the card back and scribbles an address on the back of it.

COLLEEN. You'll find the Ferret at this location, next Monday, about three a.m. And don't forget the password - you'll need it to identify him.

He takes the card, there's a pregnant moment, they're very close, almost about to kiss when suddenly her alarm goes off.

JOHN. (jumps back). Oh Christ ! Is that the time ?

She puts on her "working" clothes (fur coat etc.) and collects her expensive leather briefcase.

COLLEEN. I have an early start I'm afraid.

JOHN looks panicked.

The BELLS of the alarm clock carry over to the BELLS of the railway level crossing.

EXT/INT. BACKYARDS JOHN & SUZI's HOUSE   DAWN   (1987).
JOHN, SUZI SGT.PRIMUS (Rod Williams) CONST.HANDLING (Jean Kittson)

The BELLS of the level crossing carry over, and another train crashes past, after which the slides on the central screen again establish the rear of JOHN and SUZI'S house.

Carrying his shoes JOHN tip-toes in through the back gate. Even the back door creaks loudly as he opens it. Dreading the confrontation to come he sneaks into the house.

JOHN. Sooz ?

He feels nothing in the bed, and curious switches the light on. SUZI is not there, and neither is much else, his face drops.

JOHN. Oh no! Not again ! Oh Christ ! (looks around) Sooz ?

JOHN goes to the phone, quickly dials "000"

JOHN. (into phone) Hullo? Police? (listens) A
Burglary. (listens)
27 Batman Street, St. Kilda. (hears
footsteps) Oh shit ! They're still here (desperate
whisper) Hurry !

He drops the phone and snaps off the light again.

In the blackout we hear the door open, there's the SOUND OF A TUSSLE.

JOHN. Got you, you bastard.

SOUND OF MUFFLED CURSES, STRUGGLING ... until eventually, triumphant, JOHN switches the light back on, and we see that he's knocked someone to the ground with a pillow slip over their head. She gets up and angrily and flings it off.

JOHN. Sooz !

SUZI. What the Christ do you think you're doing !

JOHN. Sooz - we've been burgled - the records, the toaster, the TV set are gone ...

SUZI. (packing another box of books) I know, I took them.

JOHN. What ?

SUZI. I'm moving out.

JOHN. (utterly flabbergasted) Why ?

SUZI. Because of you - sneaking back in here at dawn.

JOHN. But I had a hunch about the video tapes, I think I've found out who the Ferret is.

SUZI. I can already tell you - it wears a fur coat and walks on two legs.

JOHN. Oh, we just talked fercrissake ! She's a barmaid at "The Flogger's Arms".

SUZI. (incredulous) Oh, yes, tell you her life story did she ? Till 6am?

JOHN. Sooz, I've seen things I didn't even know existed. She ... she's even got a collection of old Christian Brother's straps that are wanted by the Paris museum! I could have been hit by one of them 25 years ago. Just think - my bottom's touched part of our national heritage.

SUZI. Your bottom will touch my hand in a minute if you don't get out of the way…

He steps aside, she takes the box of books out.

JOHN. Geezus, there was nothing between. us

SUZI. (off) Don't lie - I can smell the scented oil from here, I saw the way you chased after her in a taxi.

JOHN. (from the door, firm) Well, you're the one who told me to do
something about it ! (then weakens) Sooz … Sooz, you can't leave, please… How will I meet the house payments? Who'll iron my shirts ?

SUZI. (coming back in, packing more books) You'll have to do them yourself, John.

JOHN. But, Sooz, be reasonable. .

SUZI. Look, John, we always said we'd be honest with each other remember? That was the deal - there were no chains attached.

JOHN sighs, sits.

JOHN. Well, alright, I am attracted to her. I haven't done anything, but I am attracted, alright ? I don't find it immoral. I don't even find it all that uncommon these days …I mean why can't three people love each other ? We're adults; surely, we can live with it. Here we are at the end of the Twentieth Century, surely some rules have changed…

SUZI. I'd like to break every rule in your body!

JOHN. You can't move out, Sooz, you can't afford rent as well as the house repayments here - where are you going to stay?

SUZI. (simply) David's place.

He can't believe it.

JOHN. David Meredith's place ? !!!!

SUZI. Well, yes, why not ?

JOHN. You're screwing *him* again!?

SUZI. We share a little meditation, that's all. He lets me use his floatation tank.

JOHN. How dare you ! With that suck ! After all I went through last time !!! His floatation tank !

She calmly goes on packing.

JOHN. Look, I'll go to the pub where she works. I'll call it off immediately.

The sound of an APPROACHING SIREN.

JOHN notices something in the box of books she's packing.

JOHN. Hey - that's my copy of "Life After Marriage" *and* my "Treasury of Australian Humour" Oh god - what else have you been taking…(spots it already packed in one of her boxes) And hullo - *I* paid for the radio alarm clock!

He retrieves the books and the clock from her box and is just tucking them under his arms as the door crashes down and Sgt. Primus and Const. Handling storm into the room, guns at the ready

HANDLING. (grabbing John in a wristlock, slamming
him against the wall) Right, got one, Sarg.

The goods he's carrying drop to the floor.

JOHN. Oh no- please. No. Not the RSI elbow. I just had it treated.

PRIMUS. Strip him constable…

23. INT. JINGLE JANGLES KNIGHT KLUB   NIGHT (1987)
SUZI, JOHN, SINGER (Helen Tripp) FLOWER SELLER/COLLEEN (Jean Kittson), FERRET/WAITER (Rod Williams)

By way of apology, and out of true contrition JOHN has taken SUZI out for a slap up dinner at the local night club – the "Ye Olde Steake Pitte" at *Jingle Jangles*.

They hold hands across a candle light restaurant table while in the background
a slick combo called *Trifecta* (snare drums, solo sax, and singer) are playing that old Hollywood classic and Oscar winner "Love Is A Many Splendored Thing."

The band is just out of the spotlight, only the SINGER in her lurex ball gown and pink orchid can be seen.

SINGER. Loooove is a many splendoured thing. It's the April rose that only grows
In the early spring
It is nature's way of giving
A reason to be living
The golden crown that makes a man a
Kiiiiinnnnng
Loooove ... etc.

FADE DOWN SONG as:

JOHN. Thanks for bailing me out again.

She shrugs, they stare into each other's eyes for a moment. Maybe it's love, maybe not...

> JOHN I'll make it up to you, Sooz, I really will darling.
>
> SUZI. You always said you'd make me love you didn't you, John ? You always said that you'd be true.

He shrugs.

> SUZI. But you never said you'd love me too. That wasn't ever part of the deal.
>
> JOHN. Oh Sooz, of course, I do, there's no one else ... truely.

In the background, and throughout the scene, THE FERRET comes in, and in his shifty way, ducks behind various bits of furniture, obviously hiding from someone or something out in the street. JOHN and SUZI react to him intermittently, but it's none of their business, so they try to ignore him.

> JOHN. Love is what we're born for. It's what we're best at. It's the only thing that makes life worth living. I'd die if I thought you weren't going to be there when I got home ...
>
> SUZI. (jumping in) Cooking dinner, laying out the TV trays ...

They both SNIGGER at this veiled reference to DOTTY.

Again, in the background, the SONG FADES UP as very strangely dressed men with ambiguous anatomies dance around the tables:

> SINGER. Looooove is a many splendoured
> thing. It's the April rose that only grows
> In the early spring -
> It is nature's way of giving
> A reason to be living
> The golden crown that makes a man a
> Kiiiiinnnnng
> Loooove ... etc.

JOHN takes her hand, as a FLOWER SELLER (COLLEEN) comes in, working her way from table to table.

> JOHN. (taking Suzi's hand again) Oh, darling, it's going to be *so* good - you and me, we complement each other. And there *is* no one else truely. I swear I never even got to know her name.

Behind JOHN, the FLOWER SELLER comes up.

> COLLEEN. Flower for the lady sir?

> JOHN. (without taking his eyes off Suzi). No thanks, we brought our own.

COLLEEN. (taking a camera from around her neck) It's only for charity.

JOHN. (still without looking at her) Please go away, we're Catholics.

COLLEEN. Perhaps a photo then ?

JOHN. (finally rounding on her, annoyed) Oh Please ! Will you just (piss off !)

He freezes on recognising her.

JOHN. (his heart skips a beat) COLLEEN !

SUZI reacts, shocked. COLLEEN too, is taken aback.

COLLEEN. Jack!

SUZI. Jack?

JOHN. (introducing them) Colleen, Suzi...

The two women pointedly ignore each other.

As again the song swells. . .

SINGER. Looooove is a many splendoured thing.
It's the April rose that only grows
In the early spring-
It is nature's way of giving
A reason to be living
The golden crown that makes a man a
Kiiiiinnnnng
Loooove ... etc.

SUZI. (indicating COLLEEN's camera) That's your Pentax K1000 isn't it ?

JOHN. I told you I met Colleen when I was ah…
researching the lost tapes. . .

SUZI pushes her chair back, ready to walk out.

JOHN. (restraining her) Sooz, please …
(turning desperately to COLLEEN) Perhaps
you'd like to join us for a drink ?

But they both storm off – in different directions. JOHN is momentarily unsure which direction to follow. He heads after SUZI.

JOHN. Sooz ! Sooz ! Wait !!!

But at the door he's stopped by THE WAITER who rather sternly presents him with a bill, blocking his way.

JOHN. What ? Oh…oh…. (fumbling for his
wallet, anxious to keep moving, soon finds it's
empty) I'll ah… have to go to an autobank…

He races out. THE WAITER follows.

<u>24. EXT. AUTOBANK MACHINE   NIGHT(1987)</u>
JOHN, WAITER (Rod Williams)

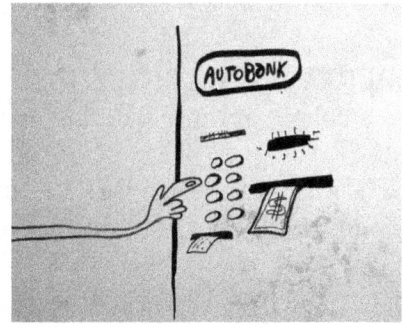

JOHN races up to the autobank machine, quickly followed by THE WAITER, who stands, menacingly over him.

Intimidated, JOHN fumbles in his wallet and quickly shoves the card in.

WEIRD COMPUTER NOISES emanate from the autobank as he quickly realises his mistake.

      JOHN. Oh no - my Ozcard !

He tries to grab it back, but it's too late. The COMPUTER SOUNDS GO HAYWIRE.

      JOHN. (bleakly turning to THE WAITER)
      Alright, I'll wash the dishes. .

25. INT. COLEWORH SUPERMARKET   DAY (1987)
COLLEEN, BERYL (Helen Tripp) JOHN, SENIOR MANAGER (Rod Williams)

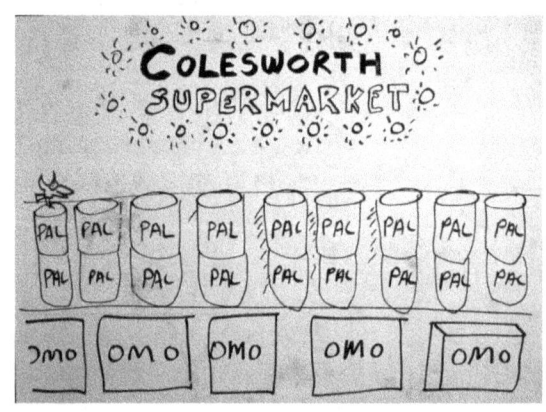

BERYL is BANGING THE BELL on top of her cash register. She pumps it a couple of times, holding up a $100 note.

COLLEEN is beside BERYL, in her fur coat, a dozen or so bottles of Johnson's Baby Oil beside her on the counter.

      BERYL. Check one hundred thank you.

More BELL RINGING.

      BERYL. Check one hundred please…

JOHN rushes in late, fumbling to put his bow-tie on. He nervously grabs for the float tin - avoiding eye contact with COLLEEN. They seem not to acknowledge each other.

> JOHN. Sorry I'm late, Beryl. I can only catch a bus now, and the stop's miles away. (counting out the change for $100). Twenty, forty, sixty...
>
> BERYL. (pointedly) Perhaps you'd like to handle this one, *personally*, yourself Mr. Smith? (with the emphasis on "personal")
>
> JOHN. (rounding on her, annoyed now) Oh shut-up Beryl !

The SENIOR MANAGER dressed in a smart suit comes up behind them, overhearing the last few words.

> MANAGER. Ah, John - could I have a word?
>
> JOHN. (sharply) I'll be there in a minute alright ?
>
> MANAGER. Perhaps you'd like to take the morning off.
>
> JOHN. (cracking) I don't need the morning off.
>
> MANAGER. Alright - well take the rest of the day then.

JOHN pulls up short, realises he's gone too far.

> JOHN. Sorry, sir, I didn't mean to yell .
>
> MANAGER. You're acting very strangely this morning Mr. Smith.

JOHN. (flinging all deference to the winds) Oh - and when you don't act strangely all the time that doesn't amount to a crack up too ?

MANAGER. I'll file your pay statement now … if you'll just give me your Ozcard - you can take a weeks wages and go !

JOHN. Ah… (just looks, at a loss)

He's stuffed.

INT. DEPARTMENT OF SOCIAL CONCERN   DAY (1987)
JOHN, SOCIAL WORKER (Helen Tripp)

JOHN is having a hard time establishing his *bona fides*. As with the BANK MANGER earlier, JOHN sits on a stool that is much lower than the SOCIAL WORKER's desk.

SOCIAL WORKER (biro poised to write) Ozcard number ?

JOHN. I don't know ! It was on the card, that's why I'm here.

SOCIAL WORKER. (shaking her head) Oooh - I dunno - that's going to be hard…

JOHN. But you've got my name an address - surely that's all you need.

SOCIAL WORKER. I can't just give a person's Ozcard number out over the desk - how do I know you're who you say you are?

JOHN. Look - My name is John Alexander Smith. I was born in Murwillumbah New South Wales on the 14th of March 1949, I live at 27 Batman Street St. Kilda...

He stops as soon as he says it.

JOHN. Well, actually, I don't ... live there anymore - we had to sell you see, cause Suzi left. All I got out of it was enough dough to buy my tapes back. (despondent) From the guy who stole them.

SOCIAL WORKER. Well - I'll try your birthplace and date, but it's highly irregular... (she's not sounding too positive)

JOHN. Thanks. I appreciate that.

She taps the information into her desk top terminal. Shakes her head.

SOCIAL WORKER. No – sorry, your bio-details aren't on the data base.

JOHN. (frowning) What do you mean ...

SOCIAL WORKER. (shaking her head) Sorry. Nup.

JOHN. You're saying - I don't exist?

SOCIAL WORKER. Our computers never make mistakes, Mr. Smith.

JOHN. So yesterday I existed, and today I don't !?

SOCIAL WORKER. If you're not in the data base that's it I'm afraid.

JOHN. That's bloody ridiculous !

SOCIAL WORKER. But efficient … It's saved the government millions. (She's looking quite pleased with the fact)

JOHN. Next time I'm voting Democrat.

SOCIAL WORKER. Look - I'll try your old address, but not with any great hope I'm afraid…

She punches in the address. Checks the screen.

SOCIAL WORKER. Ah - Now I see. Oh yes. (punches in more info)
You really did drop it in an autobank machine,

JOHN. (glimmer of hope) That's what I keep telling you!

SOCIAL WORKER. Your bio details and Ozcard number are sitting there between the grooves of a master disk pack. Could take months, even years to fish it out.

JOHN. Oh Kerrrrist!

SOCIAL WORKER. Yes, well blasphemy won't help, but you can register an appeal though. In some instances the Ministry will try and accommodate the odd anomaly.

JOHN. Great. Let's do it.

SOCIAL WORKER. (taking another file) I'll just get a few details – ahm ... Ozcard number?

JOHN just looks at her and ... SCREAMS

INT. FLINDERS STREET STATION TOILETS   NIGHT (1987)
JOHN, COMMUTER ONE (Helen Tripp), COMMUTER TWO (Caz Howard) FERRET (Rod Williams) INSPECTOR RAMSHOT (Jean Kittson) CONSTABLE McKEEN (Helen Tripp)

Slides establish an underground Gent's toilet at Flinders Street Railway station: a Gothic, echoy place with fog on the floor, and somewhere off a PLOPPING, DRIPPING TAP. Low, moody lighting.
There's already a COMMUTER ONE (Helen Tripp) at the urinal. Only 'his' back is visible: an overcoat with collar turned up. JOHN goes straight up and stands beside "him".

After a moment...

> JOHN (summoning up the courage and in a
> LOW WHISPER)
> The last train goes at midnight. .

Beside him, COMMUTER ONE reacts, shocked, moves away, leaving a gap of a couple of urinals between them before continuing his business. JOHN pushes on.

> JOHN (checking the card Colleen gave him)
> Jimmy said the tuna's due on Tuesday ...

It obviously still doesn't register with COMMUTER ONE who quickly buttons "his" fly and makes a hasty exit, with a few precautionary backward glances in JOHN'S direction just to be on the safe side. JOHN sighs, waits, more on edge than ever now.

Soon, another COMMUTER (TWO) comes in, stands up at the urinal a few feet away. John risks a look sideways at "him". This COMMUTER TWO catches the look, frowns, looks away.

Suddenly:

> JOHN. (checking the prompt card again) I'm looking for the "Last Train To Bombay" ... (no reaction from COMMUTER TWO) To Madrid ? ...

COMMUTER TWO rounds on him, spitting it out.

> COMMUTER TWO. Well you won't catch them at Flinders Street, mate !

And savagely buttons up "his" fly and makes for the door.

> COMMUTER TWO (muttering, peeved, heading out) 'Though you might catch a few other things !

Faintly in the distance somewhere above the toilet we hear the unmistakable but muffled VOICE OVER of the station's PA:

> PA (off) Flinders St. Flinders St. Port Melbourne Train Platform 11 Stand clear, please, stand clear...

After another moment or so, there's the SOUND OF A POLICE HELICOPTER hovering overhead, then a POLICE SIREN is heard approaching, just as ... THE FERRET backs in, dodging a spotlight shining in from somewhere outside. He carries an Qantas bag over his shoulder and is dressed in his usual costume of cowboy hat, shirts, boots, jeans and thin lace tie. The helicopter PASSES OVER, the sound

INCREASING IN VOLUME and then FADING as the FERRET dodges behind a few pillars and finally makes his way to the urinal. Where, after a couple of false starts. JOHN finally has another go:

> JOHN. I'm looking for the last train to Gun Hill…

THE FERRET looks at him sharply for a moment, so JOHN thinks he's made another mistake - until THE FERRET quickly grabs him, pulls him over to a hand-dryer, and hits the button to turn it on - to effectively to cover their voices.

> FERRET. Is it a passenger or goods train ?
>
> JOHN. Goods!
>
> FERRET. Platform 13, goes at midnight.

THE FERRET lets him go and for the first time JOHN relaxes.

> JOHN. Thank god for that.

> FERRET. You've got the parcel ?

John hands him a plain coloured envelope.

> FERRET (quickly counting the contents) I'll make sure it goes first class.

He hands JOHN a parcel from his Qantas bag and walks off. JOHN holds THE FERRET'S package, quickly opening it and frowning.

> JOHN. Nine hundred bucks for three tapes !

He's about to protest but pulls up short on seeing INPSPECTOR RAMSHOTT enter just as THE FERRET, head bowed, slinks past him, heading out of the toilet.

RAMSHOTT lets THE FERRET go, but retrieves the envelope from his top pocket just as he edges past. THE FERRET reacts.

> FERRET. (protest) Hey! (Then realizes who it is.) Oh sorry, mate. My mistake. (And hurries on out without his cash)

CONSTABLE MCKEEN enters behind RAMSHOTT and blocks any further exit.

In shock, JOHN drops his three tapes onto the tile floor. MCKEEN immediately scoops them up.

> MCKEEN (handing them to RAMSHOTT) Porn videos, Inspector.

> JOHN. (shocked) What ? They're supposed to be old Hollywood classics.

THE COPS laugh derisively. Heard it all before.

MCKEEN. Can you produce a receipt for these items sir? (checking the label) belonging to the ... Australian Film And Television School?

JOHN. (standing his ground) I'm the victim of several burglaries I was simply trying to get my stuff back from the thief who stole it all.

RAMSHOTT. That's our job son - don't you trust us?

JOHN. Yes, of course, but ...

RAMSHOTT opens the envelope.

RAMSHOTT Well, well, well... (holding several $100 bills up, closely examining the holes drilled through them) Condemned notes constable, you can see the holes the Australian Mint drills through them prior to burning. This is very serious indeed.

JOHN. (protesting) They were given to me by the JapHand Australasian Bank ! They're my life's savings.

RAMSHOTT hands the money to MCKEEN who puts them into a plastic evidence bag.

MCKEEN. Ozcard ?

JOHN. (slumps, how many times does he have to say it) I *lost* my Ozcard.

RAMSHOTT. I'm afraid you're wrong there, John Alexander Smith.

JOHN reacts. How do they know his name?

RAMSHOTT. Your Ozcard has just been handed back
to the Domestic authorities by the Department
of External Affairs.

JOHN'S face brightens. Hope at last.

JOHN. What ?

MCKEEN Apparently it turned up in an
extremely sensitive Defense Department
computer which immediately reclassified
Batman Street as a primary nuclear target.

JOHN. (reaching for it) Oh, thank god !

RAMSHOTT (holding it back a moment,
double checking) Your name *is* John A Smith,
of 27 Batman Street, St. Kilda?

JOHN. Yes, yes, oh yes, thank you Inspector.

JOHN eagerly takes it, glances at it, his smile of relief turns to a frown.

JOHN. But this has got a lasergram of Joh Bjelke Peterson on it.

RAMSHOTT. (snatching it back from him) Yes, and a pretty sick joke on the Ozcard Corporation if I do say so myself, Mr. Smith.

JOHN. But…

RAMSHOTT (practically ramming it against his face) Do you have any convincing explanation as to why a lasergram of the Governor General should appear on *your* Ozcard !?

MCKEEN. Are you mocking his excellency?

JOHN. No, but I wish my old man was still alive, he always said I'd never amount to anything.

28. EXT. POLICE STATION   NIGHT (1987)
JOHN, SUZI, CONSTABLE MCKEEN (Helen Tripp)

JOHN staggers out of the Police Station. It's late. He looks totally disheveled. Washed up.

>SUZI. John ! (distastefully) They said you were arrested in a male toilet.

>JOHN. (laughing/ almost hysterical) Yes ! But they couldn't hold me because they can't find my Ozcard ! Ha ha I don't exist I'm a figment of my own imagination! (LAUGHS)

MCKEEN exists from the police station behind them, handing JOHN back his video tapes.

>MCKEEN. Inspector says you can have these back. We've got better dubs already.

SUZI frowns at the titles as he takes them.

>SUZI (reading off titles) "Gym Mistress and the Virgin Tank Commander" ??!

>JOHN. It was supposed to be "Last Train To Berlin."

>SUZI (even more amazed) "Going Ga Ga with Gayle from Grong Grong"

>JOHN. (weakly) At least it's made in Australia.

She looks at him pathetically.

>SUZI. Good-bye, John.

SUZI hands him back the tape, turns to go.

>JOHN. No - wait a minute – Sooz - it's all been a terrible mistake.

SUZI. Yes it has, (sadly) The whole seven bloody years.

And she's gone, he's stunned. Left hanging there.

JOHN. No, Sooz, wait - darling, please...

29. EXT. ROBE STREET   NIGHT (1987 - 1999)
JOHN, SHADOWY FIGURES (Caz, Helen, Jean)

JOHN staggers along Robe Street against a background of nightmare images of St. Kilda at night: drug dealers and their client addicts, ladies of the night and their client boys from the suburbs, football revelers, punks, drunks, hasbeens and wannabes. Along the empty shop fronts homeless people are rugged up against a bitter south westerly blowing straight off Antarctica...

As he walks JOHN changes gradually from his normal, assistant supermarket manager clothes into the rags we first saw him in on the railway line at the beginning.

Various "sirens of the night" reach out to him:

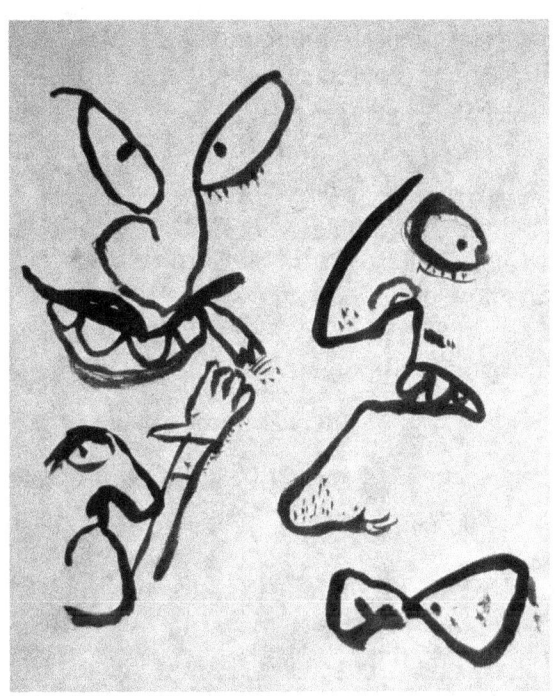

> SHADOWY FIGURES. (randomly, almost pulling JOHN towards them)
> Want to buy a girl, love?
> Well Hul-lo cowboy…
> Want to have some sex?
> Need some fun, lover boy?
> That a gun in your pocket or you just pleased to see me…

He shrugs them off, staggering gradually into his derro gear: old duffle coat, odd boots…

> JOHN. (interior VOICE OVER) Everywhere I went people were staring, laughing, clutching … and all I could see ahead was an endless, jobless wandering of streets, looking for single rooms in one night stands with holidays at the thousand star hotel…

Gradually he becomes aware of someone following him. Another SHADOWY FIGURE who stops when he stops and turns when he turns...huh?

> JOHN (continued) and always this bastard following me. I staggered up the long slow Calvary of Fitzroy Street towards the station. I knew now only one thing was certain, I had to get out of St. Kilda and fast. The clock was just striking midnight, there was one more train to go...

Images of a railway clock, and the top of Fitzroy Street, outside the old St. Kilda station. As he gets closer his "junkie shuffle" gets faster

The clock starts CHIMING MIDNIGHT.

<u>30. EXT ST. KILDA STATION</u>   MIDNIGHT (1999)
JOHN, SUZI, COLLEEN, DOTTY, STATION MASTER (Rod Williams), NORM

As the MIDNIGHT CHIMES continue, JOHN reaches the ticket gate, breathless from his exertions - only to be confronted by an old STATION MASTER padlocking it.

> JOHN. (confused) What's going on ?

STATION MASTER. Sorry mate, station's closed.

JOHN. But I've got to get out, I've got to *leave* this place.

STATION MASTER. Last train to St. Kilda's just pulling in now...

THE SOLO SAX THEME returns, picking up the slowing beat of the last train as it comes to a halt.

PA (off) St. Kilda Line ... St. Kilda Line ... Last train arriving now. Stand Clear, please, stand clear.

JOHN. Oh no-

He turns sadly away from the gate.

SUZI. John -

SUZI is just getting off the train in a halo of light that seems to glow all around her - ethereal, otherworldly.

JOHN. (a lump in his throat) Sooz !

He looks as if watching a ghost. Her jogging outfit carries the St. Kilda football team's insignia (red white and black) a halo seems to glow behind her head.

JOHN. (awestruck) Sooz, you look ... beautiful. Like some heavenly vision.

SUZI. Well yes. I should hope so. Didn't you realise ? I was the spirit of St. Kilda.

JOHN. Was ? (then realises) Oh yes. I see, yes – You, you lost the railway line … the spirit … of the place.

SUZI (dejectedly taking off halo and throwing it away – like a Frisbee) So I suppose I don't need these halos anymore.

JOHN. Oh Sooz - I always loved you.. . .

SUZI. I know, John, and I always loved you.

He goes to embrace her

JOHN. Oh darling…

When he's stopped by a THIRD VOICE.

COLLEEN. And I loved you too John.

He turns open mouthed to face COLLEEN who's also getting off the train dressed now as an angel.

JOHN. Colleen !

COLLEEN. Yes - I was your guardian angel, John.

JOHN. (can't believe his luck) Gosh ! This is fantastic. There *is* an afterlife ! I truly am in heaven.

The two women stand arm in arm, comrades together, happy, smiling back at him. Embracing him with them, including him …

SUZI. Well you are on the corner of Fitzroy Street, and Canterbury Road.

COLLEEN. Which is as close to heaven as some of us get.

SUZI. Trouble is - your suicide, you see.

COLLEEN. Yes, that was my greatest failure. Sorry, John, I tried, mate. But that decision to kill yourself - that was your one big mistake.

A fraction uncertain he detaches from the loving trio.

JOHN. But - but you've got to look at it through my eyes. I thought I'd lost both of you. All my money had holes in it. My life felt like a ping pong ball sliding down a clown's throat.

COLLEEN. We know, that's why you're here.

SUZI. All those problems are behind you now.

COLLEEN. Because we love you John (turning to SUZI renewing their embrace) and we love each other.

JOHN. Oh wow ! Oh thank you. But hang on (struck
by a disturbing thought) - wasn't St. Kilda a
bloke ? A monk or something on some remote
Scottish island.

DOTTY appears in a monk's habit - also getting off the last train.

DOTTY. That's right, John. I am that man, and
I love you too.
(embracing him - making it now a smiling,
loving quartet)

JOHN senses a tinge of danger, eyes darting around, pinching himself just to see if he is really awake.

JOHN. Hang on – (pinches harder) I ... I can't
actually feel anything.

Finally NORM appears dressed in his perennial pajamas and slippers.

NORM. (going to rub his leg) That's alright,
son, I'll get that feeling
back - cause even I love you now ...

JOHN'S mouth drops, eyes bulging. NORM embraces him, hugging him affectionately.

NORM (voice over) Love you now ... love
you now ... love you now.

His ECHOING VOICE reverberates over the noise of THINGS CRASHING...

JOHN shrinks back, horrified.

BLACKOUT

Slides ripple dissolve through to:

31. EXT. ST. KILDA STATION   DAY (1999)
JOHN, SUZI, HARRY THE BROOM

JOHN is lying sprawled out across the railway line where it all began. HARRY THE BROOM is shaking his leg, stirring him awake.

>HARRY. I leave you now…
>
>JOHN (asleep) No- please!
>
>HARRY. I said *I leave you now!!*

JOHN is retreating, holding his hands up protectively, covering his face.

Just as SUZI jogs up along the railway line, still wearing her St. Kilda footy gear. A stop watch hangs from around her neck. She reacts to the sight of the two elderly, derelict men apparently embracing each other.

>HARRY. Can't lie around sleeping with you all
>day.

JOHN quickly scrambles to his feet as if nothing had happened. HARRY pushes his bins off.

>JOHN. Sooz !

She grimaces as she confronts the shambolic figure scrambling to his feet in front of her. She's about to give him wide berth preparing to jog on.

        JOHN. Sooz ! It's me … John - John Smith.

She frowns, stops her watch.

        JOHN. Don't you remember me ?

        SUZI. (shocked) John! God you shithouse.
        What are you doing here?

        JOHN. Oh – I still live here. Here and there -
        out and about … well out mostly. Alfresco.
        Camping holiday. Thousand star hotel.

        SUZI. (cutting to the chase) On the streets …

JOHN. (smiling self consciously) It's a living.

SUZI. Not bad weather for it.

Sound of DISTANT THUNDER.

JOHN. Actually, I'm trying to kill myself.

SUZI. (clicks her watch again, about to run on) Oh well, good luck.

JOHN (stopping her, stunned) Hang on - "good luck " Is that it ? After seven years living together? Good luck ?

SUZI. That's what you'll need if you're going to kill yourself here, John. This is the old St. Kilda line.

She makes another attempt to jog on. Again he restrains her.

JOHN. I just wanted you to know you were right. Life isn't really important, it's what you *do* with your life. People who are organised are always so vital, so energetic, so ALIVE ! (getting worked up, pumping his fist in the air)

SUZI (sniffs) What's that smell.

He sniffs, checks under his boots, then realises there's a squashed dog turd on his coat

JOHN. Oh no- bloody dogs .

SUZI (recoiling) You smell worse than a footy crowd.

JOHN (shrugs) Beggars can't be choosers.

SUZI. That's all gone as well, thank god. 'Least the parking's a lot easier round here on Saturdays.

JOHN. What ?

SUZI. The footy club. Gone.

JOHN. What, the Seagulls? Flown?

SUZI. (nods behind her) Up to Darwin. They're the Crocodiles now.

JOHN. That's incredible. They can't do that !

SUZI. (moving off again) Sorry- I'm up against a stopwatch myself.

Again he has to almost physically stop her. Holding her back, pleading.

JOHN. But Sooz, they can't do this to us mate. First our train and now our footy club!? It's just not on.

SUZI. (pulling away from him) Sorry - you're about 12 years too late .

She starts her stop watch and jogs off.

JOHN. It's never too late ! They might've stopped the train, but it's not gone forever ! The rails are still here aren't they? We'll make 'em rebuild the bridge! We'll get a Melbourne sponsor to buy back the seagulls team ! TOMORROW IS OURS ...

He stops, catches himself, crouches low, bending over, holding himself in. Almost about to throw up.

>JOHN Oh no … (slow dawning realisation as he picks
>up his air mattress, clutching it to him,
>stopping himself from vomiting)
>Oh god! (aghast)
>I've got a reason to live!

BLACKOUT.

CURTAIN CALL

Jean Kittson, Helen Tripp, Paul Davies, Caz Howard, Rod Williams

CRITICAL RECEPTION

The Melbourne Age

Life on MetRail's chopping block

REVIEW

Theatre

LEONARD RADIC

Last Train to St Kilda? by Paul Davies (TheatreWorks, 14 Acland St, St Kilda)

IF topicality was all that went to the making of a good play, TheatreWorks would be on a certain winner with 'Last Train to St Kilda?'. Unfortunately, other qualities are called for; and Paul Davies's script does not have them.

In his earlier environmental plays for TheatreWorks — 'Storming Mont Albert by Tram', 'Breaking Up in Balwyn' and more recently 'Living Rooms' — he revealed a wonderfully inventive streak. The novelty lay not so much in the scripts themselves as in the sense of occasion created by playing them on a tram, a Yarra riverboat, and inside an historic St Kilda home respectively. This was community theatre at its best.

Ideally, the new play should have been staged aboard a St Kilda red rattler but the Government got in early and closed the line, leaving TheatreWorks with no choice but to stage the play in a conventional theatre format. In that environment, I am afraid, it looks thin and dramatically undernourished.

It begins brightly enough with the author, cast in the role of a local deadbeat, lying on the St Kilda railway tracks, waiting for a train to come and end his misery. Alas for him, the year is 1999, and the line has been closed for 12 years. As the broom-wielding Harry drily observes, "next time try the Frankston line, mate". There, at least, the trains still run.

From this point, the play flashes back a few years to tell the story of our deadbeat hero and the traumatic seven years that he spent mortgaged to the hilt in a renovator's dream in St Kilda with his bank-teller partner Suzi (Caz Howard), a refugee from landlocked Brunswick.

Their life together is a catalogue of disasters. They are robbed at auction, burgled on their first night in the suburb, harassed by the police, and burgled again. To cap it all, our hero loses his Auscard and is left without supportable identity of any kind. "Life's a bitch", he decides as he lays his head on the Rail chopping block.

The play is an attempt to ma number of concerns on the author' — in particular, his concern for the vidual in a society controlled by bu crats and threatened by develope

The trouble with this approach i his hero seems to be his own enemy. He is not in any real se victim of "progress" or "developm His loss of identity is of his own ma

In short, the play is strong on h but weak on sociology and analys can't make up its mind whether St should be celebrated for its uniqu or condemned for its seaminess. It bet both ways.

Davies himself turns in a am performance as the hapless hero Howard is effective as his par caught in a web of circumstance, other three players — Jean Kittson, en Tripp and Roderick William share a dozen and more other q change roles between them, breat life into most of them.

Denis Moore's production is paced at the start; but after interva labored script slows it down. By the it reached its destination the jokes a police harassment, burglary and cards had worn thin.

The Melbourne Times

Arts and Entertainment
Should veer more from the tracks

LAST TRAIN TO ST KILDA
Theatreworks
14 Acland Street
Review:
CHRIS BOYD

THEATRE

THERE is something primitive and raw in St Kilda that no harbour redevelopment could ever hide. There is a subculture that can't be tamed.

To people like you and me, the signs of it are broken car aerials or knife scratches in our bonnets. If we're unlucky it might be a burglary or a bashing.

I guess that playwright Paul Davies was a little unsure of his motives when he penned Last Train to St Kilda. The result is partly a (light) rail against the government, and partly a reaction against the attack on our privacy from bureacracies: in particular, their misuse of computer data bases. The style of the play is Mel Brooks farce.

Last Train to St Kilda opens on New Year's Eve, 1999. We meet the hero, John A. Smith, who has just lost his job, his girlfriend, his mortgage and his self-respect.

He attempts suicide by lying on the St Kilda train line. A cleaner from the National Trust (wearing St Kilda colours, natch!) interrupts John A. Smith and tells him that the train hasn't run for 12 years.

Harry-the-broom reminisces that once it took nine minutes to get to the city, on the St Kilda line train. Now it takes four hours by car and is quicker to walk.

We learn that John A. Smith's troubles began way back when he and his upwardly mobile de facto St Kilda. Burgled as soon as they move in, the couple are harrassed by police, neighbours and local thugs.

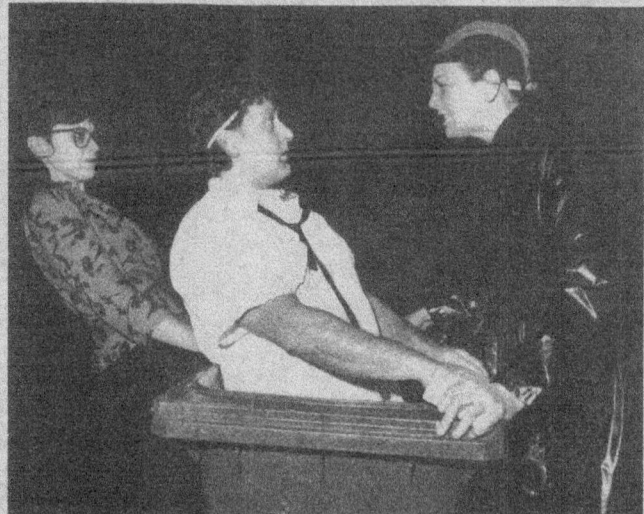

From left Caz Howard, Paul Davies and Jean Kittson play cops and harrassed citizens in Last Train to St. Kilda. Photo: RUTH MADDISON.

Unable to get insurance, they purchase an ineffective Tactical Response Man Trap. Smith's problems climax when he accidentally shoves his OZCARD into an automatic telling machine.

Suzi, the de facto, gets involved in a brawl with the Ministry for Peak Hour Traffic in her bid to save the St Kilda line train.

John A. Smith is played by the playwright, Paul Davies, and Suzi by Caz Howard. Another 20 roles are shared by Jean Kittson, Rod Williams and Helen Tripp. I can't praise these three too highly. They're wonderful.

Davies certainly has some brilliant ideas and makes some razor-sharp observations on contemporary life — like Pappelino's singing pizza delivery service — but for each classic line there are a dozen cliches. Denis Moore is responsible for the manic-pop-thrill pace and Greg Carroll for the design. Liz Pain deserves a mention for her excellent lighting.

Although for me the whole is less than the sum of the parts, Last Train to St Kilda might appeal to lovers of farce or local activists who need some comic relief.

The Star Observer

Helen Tripp, Roderick Williams, Jaen Kittson, Paul Davies, Caz Howard

St Kilda's a Star
by Chris Dobney

We may have lost our football club, the local train line is about to close and high rise hotels and marinas threaten our beloved beachfront, but old St Kilda is very much the star in TheatreWorks' new show *The Last Train to St Kilda*.

TheatreWorks collective member Paul Davies has written three plays with the company, and *St Kilda* will be the fourth. The other three have all been "location pieces", which is to say they have taken place on a tram (*Storming Mont Albert by Tram*), a suburban home (*Breaking Up in Balwyn*) and a mansion (*Living Rooms*). This will be the first play he has written for a theatre. I spoke to him about the experience.

How have you gone about this. Have you tried to reproduce the environment of St Kilda in the theatre, or have you first treated it has an open space?

I wrote the play like a film, with thirty short scenes taking place all over St Kilda, and the intention was to use slides as background to make it immediately obvious where the action was taking place. And also, because the train was closing down, I wanted to get a visual record of it. We couldn't afford to do that, so we've opted for a background of a series of cartoons shot onto slides and projected, a simple set and simple props. Everything is black and white; sets and costumes and slides. I've gone to the opposite extreme of, say, *Living Rooms*, which involved fairly loud scenes, all taking place in the same space.

So what's the format of the play — is it a whole series of snippets, or what?

It's basically the story of this very ordinary bloke, a junior assistant supermarket manager, who comes to live in St Kilda with his girlfriend. They're almost immediately burgled several times, and eventually he loses his Australia Card when he puts it in an autobank machine. He has some kind of nervous breakdown, as a result of losing his possessions and his identity and his job. The bloke, John Smith, who represents a new kind of person moving into St Kilda - a kind of lower middle class person - tries to kill himself by lying across the St Kilda railway line, only to discover that the trains have all been cancelled. It's basically his story. It's like a naive character suddenly coming into a much more cosmopolitan environment.

And have you tried to represent that cosmopolitanness?

Yes. I've only got five actors, but apart from that main character they all play lots of different roles. So we've got an underworld scene set in the Floggers Arms Hotel, which is where all the burgled goods turn up. He decides to fight back and is drawn into the underworld. He goes to the pub to try and retrieve his stolen goods and falls in love with the barmaid, so his other relationship collapses. He ends up in a male toilet and is arrested for receiving porn videos, thinking they are his precious collection of old Hollywood videotapes. It's all a terrible mistake, but he's arrested anyway.

So St Kilda is presented like a concrete jungle.

Yeah. But it's all below the surface. There's also a sort of superficial suburban normality. You know, I think Acland St and Fitzroy St are like night and day. There's the sedate, safe Acland St, and Fitzroy St represents the other side, the dangerous nightlife side. He goes from the Acland St into the Fitzroy St side. I mean it's a progression from innocence into corruption, an awareness of an older St Kilda and a kind of criminal underclass.

You don't think that all that's been cleaned up now, been sanitized.

Yeah, well there have definitely been attempts to do that, but I don't think they'll ever entirely succeed. While there continues to be a need for a place like that I think St Kilda will continue supplying it. I wouldn't like to see it entirely cleaned up, but I do object to being burgled all the time.

What other elements of St Kilda are you drawing on?

Well the train, the trainline itself. The fact that they are closing it down seems to me to reflect the changes that are happening here, the attempts to turn it into another Surfer's Paradise.

What are the characters like?

Except for the central character, who is very normal, they are all pretty eccentric. There's an element of farce to it. It's like taking an apathetic person and showing the pressures that make them develop some kind of political and social awareness.

So, in fact, he loses his official identity but learns a lot more about his personal identity.

Yes that's a nice way of putting it, there's a nice irony in that. It ends on a relatively optimistic note in terms of him wanting to fight back. I do think that with the current situation in Australia, where everything is becoming increasingly homogenized - you know, you've got the media owned by a relatively small number of people and so on - I think it's incumbent upon writers and artists to give a voice to the alternatives. That's what we're trying to do with this play.

We've been talking about it in very serious terms, but I imagine it's going to be a very funny play.

Yes, it's a very black comedy, or black and white. It's an exaggeration of the norm. What's funny I think is taking this very normal person and putting him in very extreme circumstances and letting him flounder there. It's a bit like Chaplin - a guy who is trying to maintain his dignity, even though there are holes in his shoes. As a writer I'm also very heavily influenced by people like Joe Orton and Dario Fo. They both have a political consciousness, and are able to use humor to make valid points about the hypocrisies of straight society. I think that's another thing that theatre can do. By holding up a mirror which makes people laugh at the absurdities you in fact get them to rethink the priorities.

So are our gay readers who are also St Kilda dwellers likely to see themselves reflected back in this mirror do you think?

I hope that they identify with the situations, yeah. I haven't attempted to include a "token" gay character, if that's what you mean, but it could be that some of the characters are gay. I mean, I can't speak for their sexuality; they'll have to come out for themselves.

Last Train to St Kilda by Paul Davies performed by TheatreWorks Commences: Friday 7 August at TheatreWorks, Acland St, St Kilda

Australian Visitor News

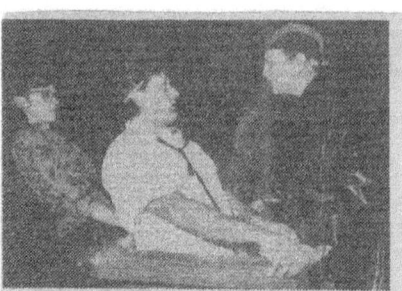

From left Caz Howard, Paul Davies and Jean Kittson play cops and harassed citizens in Last Train to St. Kilda.

NEEDS TO VEER MORE OFTEN FROM THE TRACKS

THERE is something primitive and raw in St Kilda that no harbour redevelopment could ever hide. There is a subculture that can't be tamed.

To people like you and me, the signs of it are broken car aerials or knife scratches in our bonnets. If we're unlucky it might be a burglary or a bashing.

I guess that playwright Paul Davies was a little unsure of his motives when he penned Last Train to St Kilda. The result is partly a (light) rail against the government, and partly a reaction against the attack on our privacy from bureaucracies: in particular, their misuse of computer data bases. The style of the play is Mel Brooks farce.

Last Train to St Kilda opens on New Year's Eve, 1999. We meet the hero, John A.Smith, who has just lost his job, his girlfriend, his mortgage and his self-respect.

He attempts suicide by lying on the St Kilda train line. A cleaner from the National Trust (wearing St Kilda colours, natch!) interrupts John A. Smith and tells him that the train hasn't run for 12 years.

Harry-the-broom reminisces that once it took nine minutes to get to the city, on the St Kilda line train. Now it takes four hours by car and is quicker to walk.

We learn that John A.Smith's troubles began way back when he and his upwardly mobile de facto were seduced into living in St Kilda. Burgled as soon as they move in, the couple are harassed by police, neighbours and local thugs.

Unable to get insurance, they purchase an ineffective Tactical Response Man Trap. Smith's problems climax when he accidentally shoves his OZCARD into an automatic telling machine.

Suzi, the de facto, gets involved in a brawl with the Ministry for Peak Hour Traffic in her bid to save the St Kilda line train.

John A.Smith is played by the playwright, Paul Davies, and Suzi by Caz Howard. Another 20 roles are shared by Jean Kittson, Rod Williams and Helen Tripp. I can't praise these three too highly. They're wonderful.

Davies certainly has some brilliant ideas and makes some razor-sharp observations on contemporary life — like Pappelino's singing pizza delivery service — but for each classic line there are a dozen cliches.

Denis Moore is responsible for the manic-pop-thrill pace and Greg Carroll for the design. Liz Pain deserves a mention for her excellent lighting.

Although for me the whole is less than the sum of the parts, Last Train to St Kilda might appeal to lovers of farce or local activists who need some comic relief.

The Australian

Theatre

Red signals for the last t

**The Last Train to St Kilda
by Paul Davies
Theatreworks
St Kilda, Melbourne**

HELEN THOMSON

THIS lively theatre company has won a deservedly high reputation for its innovative experiments performing in unlikely venues, such as a Melbourne tram. Their permanent home in St Kilda made Paul Davies' play *Living Rooms*, charting the chequered history of one of St Kilda's 19th century mansions, a fascinating exercise in local history and consciousness-raising.

Theatreworks has identified itself with St Kilda's older and predominately working-class inhabitants who view the rapid gentrification of their suburb and the developer's plans for a high rise seafront, with total dismay. The tide is running strongly against them and the closing of the St Kilda railway line on July 31 this year seems to sum up both the direction and the inevitability of changes already well underway.

I wish I could report that *Last Train to St Kilda* possessed an excellence which would represent a powerful blow for their cause. Unfortunately it is seriously flawed, possessing a committed sincerity it is true, but requiring a much higher degree of porfessional competence, both of writing and production, if it is to lay claim to any artistic effectiveness.

The simple plot takes us through the experiences of two young people who settle in St Kilda, only to find their lives gradually disintegrating under the constant onslaughts of crime and violence. The compensations of community caring are both inadequate and ambiguous. The characters consist of a series of crude stereotypes with about as much complexity as a comic strip (there are a few good jokes). The police are gun-happy fools persecuting the innocent and failing to deal with the criminals.

Somehow or other the criminals manage both to devastate the repeatedly burgled lives of the two main characters and also turn out to be the good guys in the end. Moral relativity rules in this very confused piece which simplisticly makes villains of all representatives of authority yet also makes us laugh at the culturally impoverished lives of the resident for whom it apparently speaks.

Last Train To St Kilda fails to demonstrate a real alternative to the ills it deplores; in fact, it tends to reinforce the worse prejudices about St Kilda, depicting it as a suburb so hopelessly crime ridden that any change could only be for the better.

The play itself consists of a sequence of simple scenes and lacks both structural and subtextural complexity.

Carolyn Howard, a fine actress, manages to invest her role with a convincing sincerity despite the play's shortcomings. Paul Davies as the representative Everyman, John Smith, fails to evoke much sympathy for a character barely in charge of his own life, apparently as confused as the audience ends up being after watching his play.

BEAT Magazine

Last Train to St. Kilda - (l-r) Helen Tripp, Roderick Williams, Jean Kittson, Paul Davies and Caz Howard.

Melbourne Herald (Friday Magazine)

How to rail against fate in Brave New St Kilda

Off the rails. It's something the embattled Melbourne commuter can relate to.

So it seems appropriate that the new production at Theatreworks' *Last Train To St Kilda?* opens tonight.

The play is a comic trip through life in St Kilda in the 1990s. John Smith is a "decent, ordinary bloke" who has fled the eastern suburbs and migrated to St Kilda. He is in search of a more exciting life, spent with more tolerant folk.

But things don't go well for John. He loses his job and girlfriend, his home is burgled and he ceases to legally exist when the automatic bank teller swallows his Australia Card.

It's enough to make you want to end it all, no? Yes, says John, and heads off to commit suicide on the St Kilda railway line.

But when you're on a downer, you're on a downer.

How can you commit suicide on a railway line that has been closed for 12 years?

John is joined by a bevy of other characters. (It makes the dialogue more interesting). There is Colleen, a graduate of the School of Hard Knocks, barmaid, masseuse, flower girl and criminal.

How to go off the rails in St Kilda.

There is The Ferret, burglar, money launderer, and permanent fixture at the Floggers Arms Hotel.

And there is that delightful couple, Norm and Ditty Drinkwater. They came to St Kilda 30 years ago for a two-week holiday and never left.

Last Train To St Kilda? was written by Paul Davies, author of *Storming Mont*

Albert by Tram and *Breaking Up Balwyn*.

■ **THEATRE:** *Last Train To St Kild* departs tonight, 8.17 pm, and Tuesd to Saturday at the same time. Sunday 5.03 pm. Theatreworks, 14 Acland St, Kilda. Tickets: $14.90, cons. $10.90 a $7. Bookings through BASS 11500 a the theatre 534 8986.

Centre Stage

> *"In tackling burning issues of the moment, Davies and TheatreWorks are to be congratulated."*

Now, back to theatre for adults for a look at the latest crop of Australian writing. Here we had something old, something new, something borrowed and something blue, as the old cliche goes.

The new comes from TheatreWorks in St.Kilda, as is most often the case. This is resident writer (and founding member) Paul Davies's latest piece of inventive "local" theatre, **Last Train to St.Kilda?**, a whacky look at what St.Kilda (and, by extension, perhaps, the nation) might be like in a decade's time. This is a time when everybody has to carry an ID card (needless to say, the much-discussed Australia Card) in order to be a real person. Needless to say, the central character (John A. Smith, played with suitable panache by the author) loses his Ozcard after one of the many house-burglaries he suffers as a new resident in the sleazepits of St.Kilda. He thus ceases to exist, becomes depressed and tries to kill himself on the old railway track. But, alas, the train doesn't run anymore: it's been replaced (fact: it happened just before opening night!) by something euphemistically called the "light rail" line.

In tackling burning issues of the moment, Davies and TheatreWorks are to be congratulated. However, **Last Train to St. Kilda?** is not the company's greatest triumph. It's a very funny piece and it's well served by Denis Moore's inventive and energetic production, by a good cast and by good visuals supplied by La Mama veteran Greg Carroll's set and by Barry Dickins' quirky slide projections. But there are distinct problems with the play: its awkward structure (which begins at the end and flashes back to the less interesting events leading up to it) and its tendency to take on more issues and themes than it can develop with any thoroughness render it an enjoyable punchy, vigorous but ultimately evanescent piece.

Emerald Hill, Sandgate & St. Kilda Times

From "TIMES" Emerald Hill, Sandgate & St. Kilda, Vic.

28 MAY 1987

Off the track

OKAY. You've seen the video, heard the speeches, read the brochures, been part of the scuffles, listened to the song — now you can see the play.

What else but the light rail battle could have prompted such a stimulus for the creative and energetic minds of the south?

TheatreWorks playwright and actor Paul Davies is the last to jump on the rail band wagon, so to speak.

The St Kilda company's next production is called "The Last Train to St Kilda?" Paul has just finished writing the first draft of the play, and, you guessed it, it's about the heavy railway line being closed down.

The play is to be a black comedy set in the future "when we assume the railway line has been closed down."

This fictional scenario has already upset local activists fighting for the retension of the heavy trains.

But we have to admit the most interesting bit to us is the hero — er, sort of — whose house backs onto the railway land.

He loses his Australia card by putting it in an autobank by mistake, his local footy team is sold to Darwin and the play ends with the man trying to kill himself — by lying on the train tracks, only to find that the trains don't run anymore.

Postscript: The Minister for Transport, Tom Roper, and other "people at the top" will be invited to the play, and TheatreWorks is plotting a special fund-raising night for anti-light rail activists.

The Melbourne Sun

*Page 10—The Sun, Thursday, July 16, 1987

A Place In The Sun

Future shock

IT is interesting to see how some people view the future.

Acland St's Theatreworks is planning a show for next month. The comedy of life in St Kilda in the 1990s is titled "Last Train to St Kilda?".

The blurb for the show, which opens on Friday, August 7, is an intriguing view of the next decade. It says: "What happens if your home is burgled three times in as many weeks and you cease to exist legally because the automatic bank teller has swallowed your Australia Card?

"How can you commit suicide on a railway line that has been closed for 12 years?

"Is $40 enough to buy a house in St Kilda?

"Who is the woman who keeps buying bottles of baby oil by the dozen with $100-notes with holes drilled through?"

The Melbourne Herald (Arts Magazine)

Saints alive and laughing

THEATRE

Last Train to St Kilda?
By Paul Davis
Director: Dennis Moore. Designer: Greg Carrol. Music: Tony Leonard. Cast: Caz Howard, Paul Davis, Jean Kitson, Helen Tripp, Roderick Williams.
At Theatreworks (14 Acland St, St Kilda) Tues-Sat 8.15 pm, Sun 5 pm. Tickets $14.90 (concession $10.90 & $7). Bookings BASS and 534 4879.
Reviewed by John Hindle

MERE mention of certain Melbourne suburbs provokes predictable responses.

Toorak, for instance, could stand for trendiness: Moonee Ponds for certain Humphries' evocations; Broadmeadows for the Broady Boys; and St Kilda for liberal lifestyles.

People who live in St Kilda often feel strongly about the suburb and its future. Something is always happening to St Kilda — the place needs all the friends it can muster.

TheatreWorks' new production, *Last Train To St Kilda?*, is an act of theatrical friendship. Set "somewhere in the near future", the play explores the suburb affectionately.

"I don't like St Kilda," says one of the characters. "I don't like the idea of it." We, the audience, hear the woman, but don't really believe her.

But when another character refers to Clayton as "the suburb you're living in when you're not actually alive," we, the audience, manage to agree entirely.

Why?

I suspect that we, the audience, are from St Kilda. At least, we were on opening night.

Last Train follows the fortunes of a young couple who move to St Kilda, buy a modest house for an immodest price at auction, move in, and are robbed during their first night in the suburb.

The police arrive. The robbed couple are treated like criminals. Guns are pointed at them — the police seem to be the most dangerous aspect of St Kilda life.

The couple continue to lose possessions (if there is *LA Law* and *Miami Vice*, surely there should be *St Kilda Theft*). Eventually, our young, put-upon hero loses his Australia Card and, no longer having an identity, decides to End It All. He lays down on the railway tracks. But the train no longer goes to St Kilda.

The show moves at a rapid pace, using a series of television-style sketches. Performances are strong — Roderick Williams, particularly, manages to make something out of each of the half dozen characters he plays.

Paul Davies, who wrote the play appears as John A. Smith, the man who has things happen to him in St Kilda, and makes the character workable and likeable.

In all, a pleasant, slight evening of humor and social satire.

The Melbourne Times

Needs to veer more often from the tracks

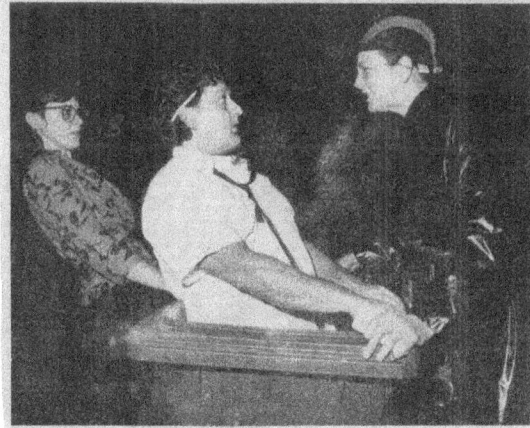

From left Caz Howard, Paul Davies and Jean Kitson play cops and harrassed citizens in Last Train to St. Kilda.
Photo: RUTH MADDISON

LAST TRAIN TO ST KILDA
Theatreworks
14 Acland Street
Review:
CHRIS BOYD

THERE is something primitive and raw in St Kilda that no harbour redevelopment could ever hide. There is a subculture that can't be tamed.

To people like you and me, the signs of it are broken car aerials or knife scratches in our bonnets. If we're unlucky it might be a burglary or a bashing.

I guess that playwright Paul Davies was a little unsure of his motives when he penned *Last Train to St Kilda*. The result is partly a (light) rail against the government, and partly a reaction against the attack on our privacy from bureaucracies; in particular, their misuse of computer data bases. The style of the play is Mel Brooks farce.

Last Train to St Kilda opens on New Year's Eve, 1999. We meet the hero, John A. Smith, who has just lost his job, his girlfriend, his mortgage and his self-respect. He attempts suicide by lying on the St Kilda train line. A cleaner from the National Trust (wearing St Kilda colours, natch!) interrupts John A. Smith and tells him that the train hasn't run for 12 years.

Harry-the-broom reminisces that once it took nine minutes to get to the city, on the St Kilda line train. Now it takes four hours by car and is quicker to walk.

We learn that John A. Smith's troubles began way back when he and his upwardly mobile de facto were seduced into living in St Kilda. Burgled as soon as they move in, the couple are harrassed by police, neighbours and local thugs.

Unable to get insurance, they purchase an ineffective Tactical Response Man Trap. Smith's problems climax when he accidentally shoves his OZCARD into an automatic telling machine. Suzi, the de facto, involved in a brawl the Ministry for Hour Traffic in her bid save the St Kilda line i

John A. Smith is pl by the playwright, Davies, and Suzi by Howard. Another 20 are shared by Jean Kit Rod Williams and I Tripp. I can't praise three too highly. Th wonderful.

Davies certainly some brilliant ideas makes some razor-s observations on con porary life — like Pa lino's singing pizza d ery service — but for classic line there a dozen cliches.

Denis Moore is res ible for the manic-thrill pace and Carroll for the desig Pain deserves a me for her excellent light

Although for me whole is less than the of the parts, *Last Tra St Kilda* might appe lovers of farce or activists who need comic relief.

The Melbourne Herald (Thursday Magazine)

SUBURBAN DRAMA STARRING THE MET

After *Storming Mont Albert By Tram* and *Living Rooms* comes Theatreworks' *Last Train To St Kilda*, another proudly parochial work celebrating life in Melbourne's eastern suburbs and marking the passing of an era.

The Melbourne Herald (Thursday Magazine cont.)

After *Storming Mont Albert By Tram* and *Living Rooms* comes Theatreworks' *Last Train To St Kilda*, another proudly parochial work celebrating life in Melbourne's eastern suburbs and marking the passing of an era.

ONE of Melbourne's more inventive theatre companies has been given new impetus by the decline of two great Melbourne institutions: football and the St Kilda railway line.

At least, that's the view of actor, playwright and founding member of Theatreworks, Paul Davies, author of *Storming Mont Albert By Tram*, a play enacted on a tram to the city, and now *Last Train To St Kilda*.

"As football declines, theatre companies are picking up," he says. "I guess our generation, now in their 20s to 40s, are more educated; we have a different idea of leisure time."

In fact, Davies thinks companies such as Theatreworks have even benefitted from the decreases in arts funding.

"We are seeing a contraction of the possibilities in other fields, like film and mini-series," he says. "Theatre is simpler to mount. Companies like ours are very lean, there are no overheads, we never lose money. That's the way to survive."

Theatreworks began eight years ago as an eastern suburbs community theatre group. Three years ago it moved to a parish hall in St Kilda and this year received its first full government grant.

Like much of the group's work, *Last Train To St Kilda* is defiantly parochial, the inspiration for the play being the demise of the St Kilda railway line (scheduled for this Saturday). However, that does not necessarily mean it is only of local interest, Davies insists.

"The more local your focus, the more universal the themes can be. You can address the great issues," he says, pointing out that Theatreworks' *Room To Move* is curently being produced in London.

"I've never accepted the cultural cringe or thought we should dilute our work to attract wider audience. I feel there is a lot more to so-called ordinary life. You look at very ordinary, very typical people like John A. Smith and you see everyone is remarkable and different, everyone's life has comedy and tragedy."

To Davies the passing of the St Kilda railway line represents the end of an era.

"The train changed this suburb from a sleepy aristocratic village, now we see another change as they try to gentrify, sanitise and clean up St Kilda," he says.

"It's the oldest railway line in Australia — 130 years old — so it seemed important to celebrate and record its end. The line opened in great controversy because people were worried it would close off the streets and now it's being shut down in new controversy.

"There has been a very organised resistance movement, especially from disabled people who have been particularly militant because they believe they won't have good access to light rail."

The play also touches on themes Davies had been developing in another play he was working on about burglaries.

"It was about moving to the more tolerant, exciting inner city and finding the underworld. It's quasi-autobiographical. I've been robbed twice since I moved to St Kilda and so has the company. Our first night's takings in this theatre disappeared after interval because the front of house person had to work the spotlight in the second act.

"We were fairly naive and that is what this play is about; people coming up from the eastern suburbs into another world."

Davies, who grew up in Queensland watching the destruction of Surfers Paradise, is concerned progress could destroy the suburb.

"The attraction of St Kilda is its history, its nightlife, its cosmopolitan feeling and there's a danger that mindless development will destroy that. But any kind of change, whether social or personal, is interesting dramatically."

He says *Last Train* is written like a film, very simple props, entrances, exits, "very Joe Orton or Dario Fo; quick lines and rapid changes".

"There's even a black-and-white Hollywood feel like those old films — *Last Train To Bombay*. The sets and costumes are all black and white. I wanted to capture a sense of the romance of the train."

■ *Last Train To St Kilda* opens on August 7 at Theatreworks, 14 Acland St, St Kilda, phone 534 4879.

Shout Magazine

TheatreWorks PRESENTS "LAST TRAIN TO ST. KILDA?"

A heavy rail story, by Paul Davies

What happens when you're racing to catch the last train at night and you've got no money left, so you fumble your wallet and put your Australia card in the autobank machine by mistake and lose your identity? What happens when you're burgled three times and you try to get your goods back and your house burns down? What happens when, at the end of all this, you try to kill yourself by lying across the tracks at Middle Park Station only to find all the trains have been cancelled? Improbable? Unlikely? Not so ... Towards the end of 1987, if the government has its way, Australia's oldest passenger railway line, the St. Kilda - Port Melbourne service, will close. Theatre Works intends to mark the passing of this famous train line with a passionate and darkly humourous play about life in a St. Kilda of the near future.

Southern Cross

★ ★ ★

WHAT happens if your home is burgled three times in as many weeks and you cease to exist legally because the Automatic Bank Teller has swallowed your Australia card?

How can you commit suicide on a railway line that has been closed for 12 years?

Is $40 enough to buy a house in St Kilda?

Does mortgage equal marriage and vice versa?

What exactly is the St Kilda curse?

Who is the woman who keeps buying bottles of baby oil by the dozen with $100 notes riddled with holes?

The answers to these and other inane questions can be found by catching the latest lunatic production by Theatreworks, Last Train to St Kilda, directed by Denis Moore.

The inspired team that brought you Storming Mont Albert by Tram, Breaking Up in Balwyn and Living Rooms, will present this comical journey through St Kilda in the 1990s at 14 Acland Street, St Kilda, from August 7.

For bookings and information, telephone 534 4879.

★ ★ ★

St. Kilda Times

Arts and Entertainment
Should veer more from the tracks

LAST TRAIN TO ST KILDA
Theatreworks
14 Acland Street
Review:
CHRIS BOYD

THEATRE

THERE is something primitive and raw in St Kilda that no harbour redevelopment could ever hide. There is a subculture that can't be tamed.

To people like you and me, the signs of it are broken car aerials or knife scratches in our bonnets. If we're unlucky it might be a burglary or a bashing.

I guess that playwright Paul Davies was a little unsure of his motives when he penned *Last Train to St Kilda*. The result is partly a (light) rail against the government, and partly a reaction against the attack on our privacy from bureaucracies: in particular, their misuse of computer data bases. The style of the play is Mel Brooks farce.

Last Train to St Kilda opens on New Year's Eve, 1999. We meet the hero, John A. Smith, who has just lost his job, his girlfriend, his mortgage and his self-respect.

He attempts suicide by lying on the St Kilda train line. A cleaner from the National Trust (wearing St Kilda colours, natch!) interrupts John A. Smith and tells him that the train hasn't run for 12 years.

Harry-the-broom reminisces that once it took nine minutes to get to the city, on the St Kilda line train. Now it takes four hours by car and is quicker to walk.

We learn that John A. Smith's troubles began way back when he and his upwardly mobile de facto were seduced into living in St Kilda. Burgled as soon as they move in, the couple are harrassed by police, neighbours and local thugs.

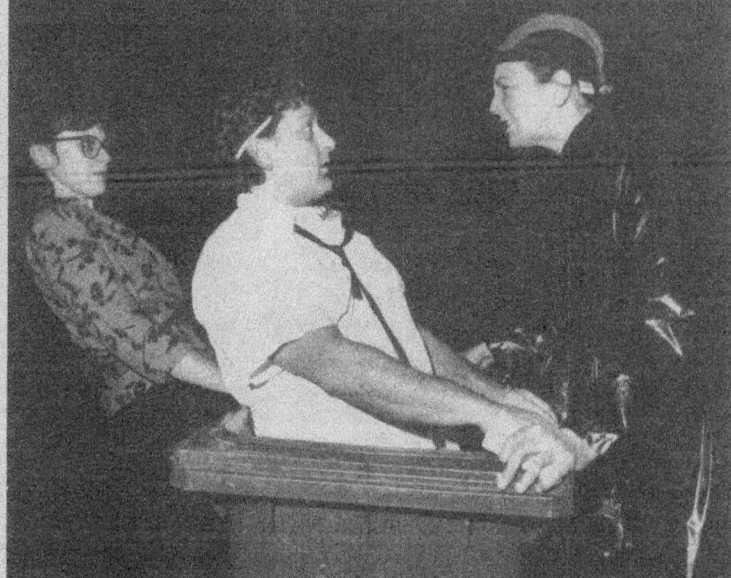

From left Caz Howard, Paul Davies and Jean Kittson play cops and harrassed citizens in Last Train to St. Kilda. Photo: RUTH MADDISON.

Unable to get insurance, they purchase an ineffective Tactical Response Man Trap. Smith's problems climax when he accidentally shoves his OZCARD into an automatic telling machine.

Suzi, the de facto, gets involved in a brawl with the Ministry for Peak Hour Traffic in her bid to save the St Kilda line train.

John A. Smith is played by the playwright, Paul Davies, and Suzi by Caz Howard. Another 20 roles are shared by Jean Kittson, Rod Williams and Helen Tripp. I can't praise these three too highly. They're wonderful.

Davies certainly has some brilliant ideas and makes some razor-sharp observations on contemporary life — like Pappelino's singing pizza delivery service — but for each classic line there are a dozen cliches.

Denis Moore is responsible for the manic-pop-thrill pace and Greg Carroll for the design. Liz Pain deserves a mention for her excellent lighting.

Although for me the whole is less than the sum of the parts, *Last Train to St Kilda* might appeal to lovers of farce or local activists who need some comic relief.

Melbourne Sun

A look at life off the rails

By GRAEME JOHNSTONE

WHAT a perfect piece of timing.

The last train will run on the old St Kilda railway line next week, and the system will shut and be replaced by the controversial light rail.

Five days later, playwright Paul Davies, the man who gave us the innovative Storming Mont Albert by Tram, will premiere his new play.

It is titled, appropriately, Last Train to St Kilda?

Davies said he had thought of the idea for the play about 12 months ago, and is quietly excited at the prospect of hitting the stage with such a pertinent piece.

In the tradition of Mont Albert — which was actually performed on a No. 43 tram travelling into the city — Last Train to St Kilda? is a suitably nutty play about the massive changes that the old seaside suburb is undergoing.

There are dual themes — the first being the closure of the railway line which Davies considers "regrettable".

"It's the oldest passenger line in Australia," he said.

"It's been getting people from St Kilda to Melbourne in a matter of nine minutes for more than 130 years.

"Now it's going to take two hours by car!

"It's a very controversial decision — even now, there are people picketing it.

"When I saw it was closing, it was too good an opportunity to miss to take a look at St Kilda in the near future."

The play is set in the 1990s — when a person can cease to exist legally because the automatic bank teller has swallowed your Australia Card.

This, in fact, happens to one of the principal characters of the play, John Smith.

Mortified by being rendered non-existent, he decides to end it all by lying down on the railway line to commit suicide — a rather difficult task when one considers the line has been closed for 12 years.

breakdown." He had even given it the working title of Invasion of Privacy.

But, once he came across the line closure story, he felt he could blend the themes together.

The burglary aspect came out of a "rather dreadful personal experience" when he moved to St Kilda to be near the theatrical company he writes for, Theatreworks in Acland St.

"I shifted from the eastern suburbs to St Kilda — and a month later all my film gear walked out the door," Davies said.

"After I had got out all the anger and frustration, we were burgled again! This time it was all our video gear.

"The first night that we made money here, in Theatreworks. — about $400 — the cashbox walked out the door, too.

"I thought I would do something about it — and about the only thing I could do is write a play."

Davies appreciates there are great changes going on in St Kilda — "an underlying gentrification process".

"It's an attempt to make it a more attractive tourist-type area, tied in with the development of the South Bank of the Yarra on the city's edge.

"The old bridge across the Yarra has to go to be part of

> It is important that development should have a human face, that it does not destroy the old values

that the older residents are not kicked out.

"We have to keep these kinds of issues before the people."

Davies said the play had a filmic quality about it — many short grabs — honed on his experience in TV and film script writing and editing.

A major part of his career was spent as a script editor at Crawford Productions, on such projects as The Sullivans and Skyways, before he joined Theatreworks and began writing plays.

The technique of staging Storming Mont Albert by Tram on a tram came about simply because the young company did not have a theatre to work in.

Having two plays about things that move on rails is not entirely coincidental. Davies is passionately interested in public transport.

His other plays, including Breaking Up in Bahqya and Living Rooms, have seen him staging his work on a boat up the Yarra.

He supplements his writing and acting with Theatreworks with freelance TV and film scripting and writing.

Theatreworks has been going for about eight years and shifted to St Kilda almost two years ago.

It has built a theatre in an old church hall at the north end of Acland St up near Fitzroy St. The group has four full-time employees and hired actors, technicians and others as each production comes up.

It has reached the point of subsistence on income from the plays, government assistance and support from St Kilda City Council. "We've never lost money," he said.

Davies will also perform in the play with Caz Howard, Jean Kittson, Helen Tripp and Roderick Williams.

Backdrop images sketched by playwright and cartoonist Barry Dickins will be used in the play, which is directed by Denis Moore.

The Toorak Times

'TOORAK TIMES' 16. AUG 87

THEATRE THAT REALLY WORKS!

The St Kilda-based theatrical troupe known as Theatre Works are currently mid-season with what I think is the funniest night's entertainment seen on stage in Melbourne for years.

"Last Train To St Kilda" takes its title from the controversial closing of the Melbourne-St Kilda rail line which, until recently had been in operation since May 13th 1857. The actual loss of the train service is a very sad one.

LAUGH TREAT

"Last Train To St Kilda" is anything but sad being a comic journey through life in St Kilda in the 1990's, and boy, you should see what the proposed Australia Card does to us in that not too distant future.

Amidst all the fun, this highly original show points out that the St Kilda line got people to the city in just nine minutes but with traffic levels still accelerating it might well take several hours by car!

Despite the title which acts as the over-riding theme, this inventive piece of modern theatre really gets down to the nitty gritty in its story of a very ordinary suburban couple caught up in the traps of modern society. The laughs come thick and fast.

ON THE RIGHT TRACK

"Last Train" is the brainchild of Theatre Works Paul Davies the man responsible for writing "Storming Mont Albert By Tram", "Breaking Up In Balwyn" and "Living Rooms", to name his most recent successes.

It's so good one wonders how long it will be before his material enters the mainstream theatre, perhaps the MTC.

And by that, I simply mean that Paul Davies' talent is too strong to be ignored; I'd like to see his shows performed all over Australia for everyone to see and enjoy.

WELL DESERVED

Paul Davies also stars in the central role in "Last Train" and featured with him is fellow founding member Carolyn Caz Howard, Jean Kittson who has worked at the Last Laugh in "Let The Blood Run Free" and "Blood Capsule"; Helen Tripp from the MTC and Roderick Williams who will be seen in the movie "Ricky And Pete".

All are excellent, as is the support of Denis Moore as director, Greg Carroll who designed the set and Tony Leonard who composed the original music for the show.

I can't recommend "Last Train To St Kilda" highly enough and having literally "froze to death" in some other theatrical locations recently, I was pleasantly surprised to find that the venue at 14 Acland Street St Kilda was cosy and warm.

Theatre-goers comforts are so sadly overlooked these days; not at Theatre Works.

Congratulations Paul, you've done it again!

Australian Visitor News

Theatreworks "Last Train to St. Kilda?"
L to R — Helen Tripp, Rod Williams, Jean Kitson, Paul Davis, Caz Howard.

Get your ticket and meet

John Smith: An assistant junior manager at Colesworth Supermarket. A decent, ordinary bloke driven off the rails.
Suzi: A health and fitness conscious bank teller. A champion of people's rights and freedoms — other than John's.
Norm & Dotty Drinkwater: They came to St Kilda thirty years ago for a two week holiday — and never left.
Colleen: Open-hearted Graduate of the School of Hard Knocks: Barmaid, Masseuse, Flower girl and Criminal.
The Ferret: Burglar, Money Launderer, permanent fixture at the Floggers Arms Hotel.

Last Train to St Kilda was written by Paul Davis, author of previous Theatreworks successes such as Storming Mont Albert By Tram, Breaking Up In Balwyn and most recently Living Rooms.

The play is directed by Dennis Moore; designed by Greg Carrol; with Music by Tony Leonard and will feature Cartoon images by Barry Dickens.

The cast includes: Caz Howard, Paul Davis, Jean Kitson, Helen Tripp and Roderick Williams.

Catch The Train at Theatreworks, 14 Acland Street, St Kilda. Opens Friday August 7th 1987. Performance times are Tuesday-Saturday at 8.17 pm, Sunday at 5.03 pm. Prices are $14.90, concessions $10.90 and $7.00. Book through Bass 11 500 and Theatreworks 534 4879. Cut price previews August 4th and 5th.

On the right track... all you need to know

Waves (SBS Radio Magazine

THEATRE

LAST TRAIN TO ST. KILDA

"Last Train to St. Kilda?" by Paul Davies
Produced by Theatre Works at 14 Acland Street
From August 6th.
Departing Tuesdays to Saturday 8.17pm (Sun 5.00pm)

In 1857 the St. Kilda railway line was built amidst great controversy. Extraordinary brawls broke out between South Melbourne council workers and the railway navvies who pushed the line through. South Melbourne Council objected to the railway line cutting off its streets. Vigorous litigation followed which was only abandoned when both sides realised it was their lawyers who were making a fortune out of it all. When the trains started running they turned a sleepy seaside village into one of the most famous places in Australia.

Now, exactly 130 years later, the St. Kilda railway line is being closed down amidst great controversy. Extraordinary brawls are breaking out between the authorities and local residents outraged at the destruction of the oldest railway line in Australia. Ironically the South Melbourne Council is leading the fight to save the line. For nearly one and a half centuries people got from St. Kilda to the City in 9 minutes. With current road traffic congestion levels it will soon take several hours. Only a society that has gone totally off the rails could even contemplate such a thing. Yet this is what will happen three days before the premiere of Theatre Works' "Last Train to St. Kilda?"

Written and produced by the same group that turned out "Living Rooms" and "Storming Mont Albert by Tram", "Last Train to St. Kilda?" deals with a society that has gone mad. A society whose opinions are formed by newspapers like the "Daily Liar", where all the money has holes in it and where, about the only thing you're allowed to get without you I.D. card is a cold sore.

It's the story of John Smith, ordinary decent bloke, a political refugee from the eastern suburb, who comes to St. Kilda looking for a more exciting, more tolerant community. Almost immediately he is burgled, he loses his job, he loses his girlfriend, and soon his whole life feels like the ping pong ball bouncing down a clown's throat. Exhausted and broke he puts his Ozcard in an autobank machine and so his loses his identity as well.

Driven to despair he tries to end it all by lying across the railway line - only to find the trains have been cancelled. What do you do when you can't even kill yourself properly? At this point he discovers that even his footy team has been sold. The local Seagulls have become the North Coast Crocodiles! This is absolutely the last straw. He resolves to fight back!

But can a mere individual Turn the Tide? Can you buy a house wit $40 in the bank? Who is the real St. Kilda and what is she the patron saint of? Can a play save a railway line?

Make sure you catch the "Last Train To St. Kilda?" and find out!

The Melbourne Age

A new play, 'Last Train to St Kilda', opens on Saturday at TheatreWorks, Acland Street (where else?). PETER WEINIGER, who grew up in St Kilda, talks to the author, Paul Davies.

Playwright rails against a dark future for St Kilda

Picture: CATHRYN TREMAIN

Paul Davies: there's still hope at the end of the line

ONE OF the memorable things about growing up in St Kilda was its accessibility, the feeling that you were living in the centre of the universe.

Everyone you knew came to St Kilda at one time or another, whether for the beach, the movies, Luna Park, the footy or Sunday lunch in Acland street. Our small flat was always full of people dropping in for coffee or a shower or the loan of a tram fare home. Friends, relatives, acquaintances, friends-of-friends, no distinctions were ever made.

We arrived in the early 1950s as European migrants, so we regarded this way of living as perfectly normal. It was only years later that we discovered most Australians lived in houses behind fences out in the suburbs, and you virtually needed a formal invitation to visit your neighbors.

My mother always kept a few cakes in a cupboard, and if people dallied she would — she still does — whip up a pile of schnitzel faster that a distant relative could utter: "I guess I'd better be getting along then . . ."

If it was easy for people to get to St Kilda — in those days families were lucky to have just one car — the abundance of public transport enabled us to travel just about anywhere in Melbourne cheaply and efficiently.

Much has changed in St Kilda since then, but some things have remained the same, thanks in part to the determination of the residents to retain the bayside suburb's cosmopolitan character, despite pressures from property developers.

The latest battle, to preserve St Kilda's rail line to the city, has been lost. The trains will be replaced by a light rail system. But their role in the evolution of St Kilda has been recorded by Paul Davies ('Storming Mont Albert By Tram', 'Breaking Up In Balwyn'), playwright with the TheatreWorks company and chronicler of life in suburbia.

His latest play, 'Last Train to St Kilda' is a black comedy excursion into the 1990s.

Mr Davis first became aware of the significance of the railway when he was writing an earlier play, 'Living Rooms',

borhood, so with the closure of the line it seemed appropriate to look at the third phase — the tourist push," he said.

The play looks at what Mr Davis calls a "lower-yuppie class" couple. He is an

"Like many newcomers, they moved to St Kilda looking for a more interesting, tolerant, cosmopolitan society, and discovered an underworld they had never anticipated — an older, darker, more primitive St Kilda", said Mr Davis.

crowded tenement, we refugees came face-to-face with our indigenous neighbors. As a kid, I remember it as an adventure rather than a shock. We got to know them and they got to know us pretty quickly. We soon overcame our dis-

ever could have from books; from down the hall took me the zoo and the Dandenongs the quiet bachelor in the be footy cards for us every we

I remember the drunks amiable. There were mutte prostitutes but I never although I fantasised a lot. can remember we were nev although our car was stolen

But back to the future, an vis's vision of St Kilda conti apocalyptic course. The q loses his job, his girlfriend his Australia Card. Deprived identity, he attempts suicid down on the railway tracks trains don't run here any m

A sense of identity — per collective — is a key eleme Davis's plays, and St Kilda's says, is threatened by devel want to turn it into the Surfer of the South. (For Mr Davis, up in Queensland, this com ominous. He still remembe when there were sand dun beach."Now it looks like Chi

Does he think his play und ticises St Kilda, which has a s ie, criminal side?

"I'm a bit of a romantic, a there is not enough roman these days, so a place like S serves to be celebrated for ness," he replied."There are identikit suburbs, so I don't t little romanticising is a bad need the kind of iconograp tricity that St Kilda provides

"I suppose I get angry at t press coverage of the darke Kilda. Sure, that exists but come a cliche for St Kilda th reflect the lifestyle of most p have come to live here. The l on that most of the trouble is outsiders and transients. If th a seamy side to St Kilda it wo be invented; every big city ha area."

He is impressed that St Ki sisted the gentrification whic taken other inner suburbs. F reason, he believes, is the way endure in St Kilda. Civilised like promenading along like t where people actually liv other. "There's terrific div around. It's a very pleased wa time, and it's free", he said.

St Kilda has always attrac and writers, and Mr Da TheatreWorks is continuing

World Theatre

WORLD OF THEATRE by ANN NUGENT

Big building union sponsors political voice to Robeson

THE STORY of the life and times of Paul Robeson, *Deep Bells Ring*, opens at the ANU Art Centre on Saturday, September 12, at 8pm.

Robeson, who died in 1976 at the age of 78, had a lifelong commitment to peace and the struggles for workers' rights. A Negro from the Deep South, he was labelled as a communist by the Committee for Un-American Activities in 1956 for his political activities. Most will remember him for his rich singing voice and film appearances (*Showboat*).

The show, with Margaret Roadknight, Jeannie Lewis and Mark Penman, is being sponsored by the Building Workers' Industrial Union in Canberra. Site performances will take place in the forecourt of the new Parliament House at 12.30pm on Wednesday (free for workers) and on Wednesday, September 16, in the Civil and Civic car park opposite Monaro Mall. ANU Arts Centre performances continue Sunday, September 13, at 4pm, Wednesday, September 16, to Friday, September 18, at 8pm and Saturday, September 19, at 2pm and 8pm. Bookings 571077.

Veronica's Room, written by Ira Levin and directed by Corille Fraser, opens at Rep's Theatre 3 on Saturday, September 12, at 8.15pm. Audiences who saw the Corille Fraser-directed *The Prime of Miss Jean Brodie* at Rep last year will be looking forward to seeing what Fraser makes of Levin's thriller.

After opening night the show runs Thursday, September 17, to Saturday, September 19, and then Wednesdays to Saturdays until October 3 with a special concession night September 17 only. Bookings 57 1950.

Last week in Melbourne I saw the Melbourne Theatre Company's production of Alan Ayckbourn's *A Chorus of Disapproval* with Max Gillies in the starring role of Dafydd ap Llewellyn, who is so preoccupied with his trials and tribulations as director of the Pendon Amateur Light Operatic Society that he does not realise his imminent marital catastrophe. Robyn Ramsay plays the highly amusing *Norman Conquest*-like character, Guy Jones, who stumbles into the tranquility of Pendon with shattering (but very funny) results. Half-price preview is offered tomorrow with opening night on Wednesday at 8pm, nightly until Sat-

In Melbourne I also saw *Last Train to St Kilda?* appropriately enough at the Theatreworks studio at Acland Street, St Kilda. The actual, as opposed to theatrical, last train to St Kilda ran on July 31, 1987, which

added a certain poignancy to Theatreworks' entertaining show. It was great to be in a community theatre packed to capacity (about 300) by an appreciative and theatre-wise audience.

hearsal Room of the Canberra Theatre Centre, Interact is presenting a rehearsed reading of Dorothy Hewett's *Chapel Perilous*.

I hear that auditions were held last weekend for Eureka's new production of the Michael Gow play, *Away*. Eureka's production, directed by Rod Charls, is scheduled for November at the ANU Arts Centre.

Coming up at TAU is Mayakovsky's *The Bath House*, directed by Domenic Mico, opening on September 22.

Over the holiday season I saw two children's plays. *I Can Dream, I Can Fly* at TAU ran for 45 minutes with a single, flat-rate ticket costing $5 and

(rector), Jeannie Lewis, Kym Ford, Chris Herden.

St. Kilda Times

Arts and Entertainment

The Emerald Hill, Sandridge & St. Kilda Times — 30 July, 1987 —

Seeing the light side of a heavy rail issue — member of "Last Train to St Kilda" cast, Jean Kitson. Photo: PETER WEAVING.

A track from Mallee to St Kilda

How does it feel to be replaced by a computer? Actress Jean Kittson knows.

After leaving college, Jean and her nifty little sportscar headed out to the Mallee to teach drama to school kids under a Country Education Program.

"In the country imagination tends to be squashed at an early age. The program was viewed as something a bit wacky," Jean recalls.

However, she loved it and soon swapped the sports car for a ute. The next year, the Schools Commission swapped the drama program for a computer program.

Oh well, you learn to take the rough with the smooth in life, especially if writing and performing are your life.

After her dalliance in the country, Jean spent a couple of years with the Toetruck Theatre Company. She then took time out to travel overseas before coming back to Melbourne, picking up a career which has turned out to be varied and exciting if not exactly lucrative.

In addition to a variety of theatre roles, Jean has appeared in "lots of Swinburne films" and quite a few radio shows.

Her latest film was *Kick Start* which took out both the Best Short Film and Best Film award at the Sydney Film Festival. It wasn't even shown at the Melbourne Film Festival.

Her latest radio project involves scripting and recording a series of *Let The Blood Run Free* for the ABC. Jean has been a member of the troupe since its inception, appearing as Nurse Pam in the recent season of *Blood Capsule* at the Last Laugh.

But it is her involvement in Theatrework's next production *Last Train To St. Kilda?* that currently takes her attention.

Jean describes the play, written by Paul Davies, as very manic. "It is stylised and it is very filmic in that there are lots of scene changes but it is really clear, sharp and quite slick," she says.

While the play is not about the rail closure as such, it is about the problems and issues plaguing the average St. Kilda resident — burglary, marriage breakdowns, mortgages, the police, the Australia Card. It is about bureaucracy and its crippling effects.

"The last train is a symbol," says Jean, "a recurring theme. The stories in it have happened to everyone.

"The play is warm and funny and a bit sad."

Jean plays a number of characters in *Last Train To St. Kilda*. One is an over-the-top policewoman, another an insurance agent and the main character is that of Colleen who is "from the school of hard knocks but still with a sense of romance" and becomes the "other woman" for the central character, John.

● *Last Train To St. Kilda* opens next Friday August 7 at the Theatreworks home, 14 Acland Street, St. Kilda. Bookings 534 4879.

KAREN BOOTH

Keilor/BroadGlen Messenger

THE LAST TRAIN FOR ST KILDA

LAST Train To St Kilda is the unlikely title of a play to be staged by Theatreworks at 14 Ackland St, St Kilda, on Thursday, August 6.

The play was written by Paul Davies, author of previous Theatreworks successes such as Storming St Kilda By Tram, Breaking Up In Balwyn and most recently, Living Rooms.

It will be directed by Denis Moore and designed by Greg Carroll, with music by Tony Leonard and cartoon images by Barry Dickens.

The characters are varied — John Smith, an assistant junior manager at a local supermarket — a decent bloke driven off the rails.

Suzi, a health and fitness conscious bank teller who is also a champion of other people's cuases, while Norm and Dotty Drinkwater arrived in St Kilda 30 years ago for a holiday and never left.

Colleen is an open-hearted graduate from the street of hard knocks and The Ferret burglar and money launderer, is a permane fixture at the Floggers Inn Hotel.

The cast includes Caz Howard, Pa Davies, Jean Kittson, Helen Tripp a Roderick Williams and the Last Train is rea a comic journey through St Kilda in the 1990

The Melbourne Report

THEATRE & DANCE

MELBOURNE REPORT
AUG / SEPT
1987

Last Train to St. Kilda? Theatreworks, 14 Acland St., St. Kilda. How can you commit suicide on a railway line that has been closed for twelve years? Is forty dollars enough to buy a house in St. Kilda? Does mortgage equal marriage and vice versa? All these questions are exposed in Paul Davis' comical journey through St. Kilda life in the 1990s. **To** Sept 6. Tues-Sat 8.15 pm, Sun 5 pm. Tickets: $14.90. Bookings: 11 500.

Paul Davies' latest play, *Last Train to St. Kilda*, at Theatreworks in August, was one of the more interesting and amusing new plays to be produced so far this year. The combined talents of Caz Howard, Jean Kittson, Helen Tripp, Roderick Williams and the playwright himself made for an excellent cast. Davies made a very good fist of acting in his own play and in fact so good was he, so charming and engaging of the audience, that one wonders if one could see a better, or even as good a production without him in it.

The play, billed as 'a comic journey through life in St. Kilda in the 1990's is ostensibly about the closure of the St. Kilda train line and the further decline in the quality of inner city life that this will give rise to.

The 'seediness' and 'local colour' of St. Kilda are drawn on to good effect in the script. The central couple are innocents abroad in a suburb seething with security fences (burglars on the inside, not the outside), paranoid trigger happy policeman, proud lovable prostitutes, pizza sellers and nosy neighbours.

This fine production was made even finer by good direction and design from Denis Moore and Greg Carroll respectively, and by a few cartoons that Barry Dickins managed to slide into the show.

◆ LAST TRAIN TO ST. KILDA
... opens August 7.

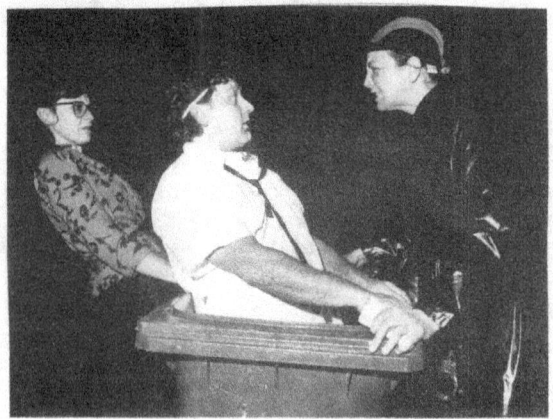

◆ CAZ HOWARD, PAUL DAVIES *and* JEAN KITTSON *in* LAST TRAIN TO ST. KILDA.

Melbourne Star Observer

Helen Tripp, Roderick Williams, Jaen Kittson, Paul Davies, Caz Howard

St Kilda's a Star
by Chris Dobney

We may have lost our football club, the local train line is about to close and high rise hotels and marinas threaten our beloved beachfront, but old St Kilda is very much the star in TheatreWorks' new show *The Last Train to St Kilda*.

TheatreWorks collective member Paul Davies has written three plays with the company, and *St Kilda* will be the fourth. The other three have all been "location pieces", which is to say they have taken place on a tram (*Storming Mont Albert by Tram*), a suburban home (*Breaking Up in Balwyn*) and a mansion (*Living Rooms*). This will be the first play he has written for a theatre. I spoke to him about the experience.

How have you gone about it? Have you tried to reproduce the environment of St Kilda in the theatre, or have you just treated it has an open space?

I wrote the play like a film, with thirty short scenes taking place all over St Kilda, and the intention was to use slides as background to make it immediately obvious where the action was taking place. And also, because the train was closing down, I wanted to get a visual record of it. We couldn't afford to do that, so we've opted for a background of a series of cartoons shot onto slides and projected, a simple set and simple props. Everything is black and white; sets and costumes and slides. I've gone to the opposite extreme of, say, *Living Rooms*, which involved thirty long scenes, all taking place in the same space.

So what's the format of the play? Is it a whole series of snippets, or what?

It's basically the story of this very ordinary bloke, a junior assistant supermarket manager, who comes to live in St Kilda with his girlfriend. They're almost immediately burgled several times, and eventually he loses his Australia Card when he puts it in an autobank machine. He has some kind of nervous breakdown, as a result of losing his possessions and his identity and his job. The bloke, John Smith, who represents a new kind of person moving into St Kilda - a kind of lower middle class person - tries to kill himself by lying across the St Kilda railway line, only to discover that the trains have all been cancelled. It's basically his story. It's like a naive character suddenly coming into a much more cosmopolitan environment.

And have you tried to represent that cosmopolitanness?

Yes. I've only got five actors, but apart from that main character they all play lots of different roles. So we've got an underworld scene set in the Floggers Arms Hotel, which is where all the burgled goods turn up. He decides to fight back and is drawn into the underworld. He goes to the pub to try and retrieve his stolen goods and falls in love with the barmaid, so his other relationship collapses. He ends up in a male toilet and is arrested for receiving porn videos, thinking they are his precious collection of old Hollywood videotapes. It's all a terrible mistake, but he's arrested anyway.

So St Kilda is presented like a concrete jungle.

Yeah. But it's all below the surface. There's also a sort of superficial suburban normality. You know, I think Acland St and Fitzroy St are like night and day. There's the sedate, safe Acland St, and Fitzroy St represents the other side, the dangerous nightlife side. He goes from the Acland St into the Fitzroy St side. I mean it's a progression from innocence into corruption, an awareness of an older St Kilda and a kind of criminal underclass.

You don't think that all that's been cleaned up now, been sanitized.

Yeah, well there have definitely been attempts to do that, but I don't think they'll ever entirely succeed. While there continues to be a need for a place like that I think St Kilda will continue supplying it. I wouldn't like to see it entirely cleaned up, but I do object to being burgled all the time.

What other elements of St Kilda are you drawing on?

Well, the train, the trainline itself. The fact that they are closing it down seems to me to reflect the changes that are happening here, the attempts to turn it into another Surfer's Paradise.

What are the characters like?

Except for the central character, who is very normal, they are all pretty eccentric. There's an element of farce to it. It's like taking an apathetic person and showing the pressures that make them develop some kind of political and social awareness.

So, in fact, he loses his official identity but learns a lot more about his personal identity.

Yes that's a nice way of putting it, there's a nice irony in that. It ends on a relatively optimistic note in terms of him wanting to fight back. I do think that with the current situation in Australia, where everything is becoming increasingly homogenized - you know, you've got the media owned by a relatively small number of people and so on - I think it's incumbent upon writers and artists to give a voice to the alternatives. That's what we're trying to do with this play.

We've been talking about it in very serious terms, but I imagine it's going to be a very funny play.

Yes, it's a very black comedy, or black and white. It's an exaggeration of the norm. What's funny I think is taking this very normal person and putting him in very extreme circumstances and letting him flounder there. It's a bit like Chaplin - a guy who is trying to maintain his dignity, even though there are holes in his shoes. As a writer I'm also very heavily influenced by people like Joe Orton and Dario Fo. They both have a political consciousness, and are able to use humor to make valid points about the hypocrisies of straight society. I think that's another thing that theatre can do. By holding up a mirror which makes people laugh at the absurdities you in fact get them to rethink the priorities.

So are we gay readers who are also St Kilda dwellers likely to see themselves reflected back in this mirror do you think?

I hope that they identify with this situations, yeah. I haven't attempted to include a "token" gay character, if that's what you mean, but it could be that some of the characters are gay. I mean, I can't speak for their sexuality; they'll have to come out for themselves.

Last Train to St Kilda by Paul Davies performed by TheatreWorks Commences: Friday 7 August at TheatreWorks, Acland St, St Kilda

The Times On Sunday

"TIMES ON SUNDAY", 23. AUG. 1987

TIMES ON SUNDAY 23 AUGUST 1987

THEATRE
BARRY OAKLEY

LAST TRAIN TO ST KILDA?, by Paul Davies. Directed by Denis Moore. Theatreworks, Melbourne.

THERE are only two people in Australia who are both professional philosophers and railway enthusiasts, and a son of mine is one of them. He was keen to come with me to *Last Train To St Kilda?*

At the start of the play, Paul Davies comes on as John Smith, a derelict. All he has left in life is a cold sore and disappointments. So he lays his portly figure across the railway line in order to do away with himself. ("Those lines are too narrow," whispered my son, "the St Kilda line is a broader gauge than that.")

But it's 1999, and a man called Harry the Broom tells him the line has been closed for 12 years. The very first passenger railway line in Australia, it was. ("Not so," said my son. "The Port Melbourne line took passengers and it opened three years earlier, in 1854.")

So we flash back to 1987, when John Smith, who's lost his memory, first came to St Kilda as an up-and-coming assistant supermarket manager to share a mortgage and a life with Suzi (Caz Howard). They are sold an over-priced house by Toecutter and Lebensraum, Estate Agents.

They are burgled three times in three weeks, and each time the police arrive before they have even been notified. Gradually Smith loses his grip on life, and when an automatic bank teller swallows his Australia Card, politically he ceases to exist. One of their few consolations is the regular, reassuring noise of the train going past.

They become friendly with Norm and Dot Drinkwater, their down-to-earth Australian neighbours, remnants of the older, working-class St Kilda. Norm is dedicated to TV and the bottle and Dot likes to extend her carpet-sweeping even to the back lawn. They all get together and discuss the Government's plan to replace the old railway with a light rail system – Suzi's against it, but her arguments are deafening rather than convincing.

If there is a central theme, this is the nearest to it. The replacement of the old and trusted by the new and doubtful is seen as symptomatic of what's wrong with St Kilda and the modern world, where decisions are made by bureaucrats and capitalists and the people affected have no say.

Though there are some funny and telling moments, and though Rod Williams, Helen Tripp and Jean Kittson make a success of most of the variety of roles they play, the writing is uneven, the structure is shaky and the scenes often follow one another jerkily.

From left: Roderick Williams, Paul Davies, Caz Howard and Helen Tripp in *Last Train to St*

Melbourne Herald (Friday Magazine)

Saints alive and laughing

THEATRE

Last Train to St Kilda?
By Paul Davis
Director: Dennis Moore. Designer: Greg Carrol. Music: Tony Leonard. Cast: Caz Howard, Paul Davis, Jean Kitson, Helen Tripp, Roderick Williams.
At Theatreworks (14 Acland St, St Kilda) Tues-Sat 8.15 pm, Sun 5 pm. Tickets $14.90 (concession $10.90 & $7). Bookings BASS and 534 4879.
Reviewed by John Hindle

MERE mention of certain Melbourne suburbs provokes predictable responses.

Toorak, for instance, could stand for trendiness; Moonee Ponds for certain Humphries' evocations; Broadmeadows for the Broady Boys; and St Kilda for liberal lifestyles.

People who live in St Kilda often feel strongly about the suburb and its future. Something is always happening to St Kilda — the place needs all the friends it can muster.

TheatreWorks' new production, *Last Train To St Kilda?*, is an act of theatrical friendship. Set "somewhere in the near future", the play explores the suburb affectionately.

"I don't like St Kilda," says one of the characters. "I don't like the idea of it." We, the audience, hear the woman, but don't really believe her.

But when another character refers to Clayton as "the suburb you're living in when you're not actually alive," we, the audience, manage to agree entirely.

Why?

I suspect that we, the audience, are from St Kilda. At least, we were on opening night.

Last Train follows the fortunes of a young couple who move to St Kilda, buy a modest house for an immodest price at auction, move in, and are robbed during their first night in the suburb.

The police arrive. The robbed couple are treated like criminals. Guns are pointed at them — the police seem to be the most dangerous aspect of St Kilda life.

The couple continue to lose possessions (if there is *LA Law* and *Miami Vice*, surely there should be *St Kilda Theft*). Eventually, our young, put-upon hero loses his Australia Card and, no longer having an identity, decides to End It All. He lays down on the railway tracks. But the train no longer goes to St Kilda.

The show moves at a rapid pace, using a series of television-style sketches. Performances are strong — Roderick Williams, particularly, manages to make something out of each of the half dozen characters he plays.

Paul Davies, who wrote the play appears as John A. Smith, the man who has things happen to him in St Kilda, and makes the character workable and likeable.

In all, a pleasant, slight evening of humor and social satire.

Also on…

F·I·R·S·T ✶✶✶ N·I·G·H·T·S

BRISBANE

August 11
As You Like It
Jim Vile is all out to make this an '87 peak for La Boite. He says he's got the right play (and he won't try to "improve" it), he's got the right forest, and he's got the right players — three-quarters of them professionals.

August 19
The Old Selection
Out of the Canberra archives where bureaucrats have had it buried for 70 years. TNI's premiere production of the new-old play by Steele Rudd. At the new-old Princess Theatre. Directed by Rick Billinghurst.

CANBERRA

Coming up in August — Eureka Theatre Company — *Salonika* by Louise Page — directed by Phil Mackenzie.

Fortune Theatre Company — Most of the company members will be taking leave but there will be a one actor, mainstage production — *The Double Bass* by Peter Suskind translated by Philip Keir. This production will be the Australian premiere of the play.

PERTH

August 25
Les Liaisons Dangereuses.
Simon Phillips returns from Melbourne for the Australian premiere of the Christopher Hampton masterpiece. Stars Michael Carman, Jane Conroy in a WATC production at the Playhouse.

August 28
The Seagull.
Hole in the Wall director Raymond Omodei has a passion for Chekhov and an eye which does not always fit with expectations. The result should be interesting. Richard Dillane is Treplev.

MELBOURNE

August 6
Last Train to St Kilda
"A heavy rail story", or (as Theatreworks writer Paul Davies puts it) an account of life in St Kilda in the 1990's, after the Australia Card's come in and the railway line's gone out. At Theatreworks, Acland St.

August 15
The Common Pursuit
The frail hopes and youthful ambitions of six people are explored in the twenty year's span of this new play by Simon Gray (remember *Butley*? *Otherwise Engaged*?) Babs McMillan directs this for the MTC at Russell St, with designer Richard Roberts.

August 17
Lily and May
As with *Cho Cho San*, Playbox have reworked something which showed potential in an earlier incarnation. This time it's the marvellous comedy by Patricia Cornelius which was a hit with Spoleto Fringe last year. Oyston directs with designs by Michael Leunig.

SYDNEY

August 1
The Golden Age.
Louis Nowra's grand analysis of what we mean by "civilisation". Convict remnants discovered in Tasmania have more to offer than their finders. Egil Kipste directs Nimrod at the Seymour Centre.

August 4
Turn of the Tide.
One Extra's most complete and exciting show to date. Mishima's sensibilities and choreographer Kai Tai Chan's experiences blend in a profusion of images. Everest Theatre, Seymounr Centre.

August 28
Every Prospect of Success.
Jolly-sounding premiere of a new play by Ted Neilsen. The founding of South Australia paralleled by present-day seekers after Xanadu. Both are ripped off. Q Theatre, Penrith.

CentreStage Australia 3

23 January 1987

Transport users want railway route changed

The Public Transport Users Association wants the State Government to revise its planned light rail lines to St Kilda and Port Melbourne and retain the present link with Flinders Street station.

The group today will lead a delegation to meet the MLA for St Kilda, Mr Andrew McCutcheon, in a late attempt to change the project before preliminary construction starts.

The St Kilda and Port Melbourne railways are due to close late this year to be replaced with double-carriage trams called light rail vehicles.

The vehicles will follow the existing railway reservations from St Kilda and Port Melbourne, but will enter tram tracks in Clarendon Street, South Melbourne instead of continuing to Flinders Street station.

They will then travel along Clarendon and Spencer Streets, turn right into Bourke Street and continue to Fitzroy and East Brunswick.

Although it does not oppose the replacement of St Kilda and Port Melbourne trains with light rail cars, the Public Transport Users Association is against the plan to sever the links with Flinders Street station.

The group says commuters strongly oppose plans to cut the Flinders Street link and that the issue could oust Mr McCutcheon — who is Minister for Water Resources — from his marginal seat at the next election.

— TONY HARRINGTON

Programme

Programme

PAUL DAVIES - PLAYWRIGHT/ACTOR

Paul was first seduced by the idea of life theatre when he won £1 in a smiling competition at the Vogue Theatre Ipswich in 1956. He came to Melbourne in 1974 to be the last script editor on HOMICIDE and the first one on THE SULLIVANS. He has since written extensively for film and television. In 1982 Paul became a full time member of TheatreWorks where he is currently employed as an actor, director, typist, cleaner, lobbyist, unskilled labourer, sometime board member and worrier. For the Company he wrote STORMING MONT ALBERT BY TRAM, BREAKING UP IN BALWYN and most recently LIVING ROOMS. As well as performing in his latest play LAST TRAIN TO ST. KILDA? he is currently working on two other projects, a film script for Welsh television based on the life of Billy Hughes and a new play for TheatreWorks under commission from the Australian Bicentennial Authority to be called ON SHIFTING SANDSHOES.

DENIS MOORE - DIRECTOR

Denis is an Honours Graduate in Arts from Flinders University and has an extensive background as a director and an actor. In the past Denis has directed plays for the PRAM FACTORY, THE ADELAIDE THEATRE GROUP and THE MELBOURNE WRITERS THEATRE as well as numerous productions at LA MAMA including a season of Jack Hibberd plays, a series of plays by Peter Mathers and most recently FITZROY CROSSING by Phil Motherwell. Earlier this year Denis directed GONE THE BURNING SUN by Ken Mitchell for THE CHURCH. As an actor Denis has performed at the PRAM FACTORY, the STATE THEATRE COMPANY OF SOUTH AUSTRALIA, the MELBOURNE THEATRE COMPANY, PLAYBOX, NIMROD and THE CHURCH.

CAROLYN (CAZ) HOWARD - ACTOR

Caz graduated from the Victorian College of the Arts in 1980. She is a founding member of THEATREWORKS and is currently a member of the artistic directorate and the Board of Directors. Caz has appeared most recently in THEATREWORKS' productions of POPULAR FRONT, CAKE and LIVING ROOMS. Her last stage performance was as Lily Doherty in FREEDOM OF THE CITY for THE PLAYBOX THEATRE COMPANY. Caz also works in independent film and video. In 1985 she played the lead in John Hughes' film TRAPS and just completed work on John's new documentary/drama LETTERS TO THE EDITOR.

JEAN KITTSON - ACTOR

Jean graduated from Rusden State College with Majors in Drama, Dance and Media. She spent two years in Sydney working for T.O.E. TRUCK THEATRE COMPANY and performing at NIMROD and the NEW THEATRE. After travelling extensively overseas for two years she returned to Melbourne to join TIME & TIDE THEATRE COMPANY to research and write GOOD TALK a women's oral history of Port Melbourne. Since the beginning of 1986 Jean's major involvement has been co-writing and performing in LET THE BLOOD RUN FREE and its successful

Programme

HELEN TRIPP - ACTOR

Helen's stage and television credits are too many and reach too far back to be recollected. Most recently she played the title role in THE DEATH OF MINNI by Barry Dickins at LA MAMA, Soot in THE MARRIAGE OF BETTE AND BOO for the PLAYBOX and Maria (McGuinness) in HEARTBREAK HOUSE for the MELBOURNE THEATRE COMPANY.

RODERICK WILLIAMS - ACTOR

After an itinerant existence in Australia and around the world Roderick began his acting career in earnest at the NEW THEATRE in Sydney. He worked with various companies in Sydney, Perth and Hobart performing leading roles in productions such as THE REMOVALIST, JUGGLERS THREE, DR. FAUSTUS, KENNEDY'S CHILDREN, THE COMING OF STORK, HABEUS CORPUS and THE BANANA BENDER and many, many others. In 1978 Roderick obtained a thirteen month contract with the MELBOURNE THEATRE COMPANY where he performed in two Australian premiers DEPARTMENTAL and MAKASSER REEF. After a serious car accident Roderick returned to the stage in 1982 in A COUPLE OF BROKEN HEARTS by Barry Dickins at the PLAYBOX. Most recently he performed in THIS IS THE WAY THE WORLD ENDS and GONE THE BURNING SUN at THE CHURCH THEATRE in Hawthorn.

Roderick's film credits include BURKE AND WILLS, WILLS AND BURKE, KANGAROO and STRIKEBOUND. His next film appearance will be as Holy Joe in RICKY AND PETE.

GREG CARROLL - DESIGNER

Greg sums up his design philosophy in three simple words – make it work. with this in mind he has worked as a designer, director and actor for various companies such as the PRAM FACTORY, PLAYBOX, LA MAMA and at the Universal Theatre. Most recently Greg directed EAT YOUR GREENS by Barry Dickins and performed in FITZROY CROSSING by Phil Motherwell.

Greg will soon appear in the feature film GROUND ZERO.

TONY LEONARD - ORIGINAL MUSIC AND SOUND

Tony has been writing and performing original music since he formed 'YASMIN AND THE TEALEAVES' in 1977, which were will known in Melbourne for their original style and unique vocal harmony blend. He is a self taught multi-instrumentalist allowing him the choice of a variety of sounds in his work.

His recording credits range from his own self-titled album to arranging for other successful Australian artists including Captain Matchbox. Tony is currently working as a composer in film and theatre and has worked extensively in radio and television.

Company "Dodger"

LAST TRAIN TO ST. KILDA?

A COMIC JOURNEY THROUGH LIFE IN ST. KILDA IN THE 1990's

What happens if your home is burgled three times in as many weeks and you cease to exist legally because the Automatic Bank Teller has swallowed you Australia Card?

How can you commit suicide on a railway line that has been closed for twelve years?

Is forty dollars enough to buy a house in St. Kilda?

Does mortgage equal marriage and vica versa?

What exactly is the St.Kilda curse?

Who is the woman who keeps buying bottles of baby oil by the dozen with $100 notes with holes drilled through?

Should the police be doing something about all this?

Should you?

FIND OUT ALL THE ANSWERS BY CATCHING THE LAST TRAIN TO ST. KILDA?!

Please turn over.....

Paul Davies is an award winning screenwriter, script editor and playwright who sharpened his quill on over a hundred episodes of Teledrama from classic Crawford series such as *Homicide* (1974-5), *The Box* (1975-76) *The Sullivans* (1976-78) and *Skyways* (1979), to *Rafferty's Rules* (1985), *Blue Heelers* (1997), *Pacific Drive* (1996), *Stingers* (1998-2003), *Something in the Air* (1999-2001) and *Headland* (2005). He also helped spark the site-specific performance revolution in Melbourne in the 1980s with TheatreWorks' production of his first play *Storming Mont Albert By Tram* (1982). What became known as *The Tram Show* played across a dozen years to packed trams in both Melbourne and Adelaide, travelling a total distance that would have taken the show halfway round the world.

TheTram Show's success lead to an outbreak of 'location theatre' in Melbourne throughout the 1980s including three other plays written to be performed in real places: *Breaking Up In Balwyn* (1983, on a riverboat), *Living Rooms* (1986, in an historic mansion) and *Full House/No Vacancies* (1989, in a boarding house).

These works became the subject of his book *Really Moving Drama*. Both *The Tram Show* and *On Shifting Sandshoes* (1988) were awarded AWGIES, along with *Return of The Prodigal* (2000) an episode of *Something In The Air* (ABC). Paul co-wrote the feature *Neil Lynn* with David Baker in 1984, and the docu-fiction *Exits* (1980) with Pat Laughren and Carolyn Howard. Paul has also worked on the scripts of John Hughes' documentaries, *Traps* (1984), *All That Is Solid* (1985), and *One Way Street (Fragments for Walter Benjamin)* (1991). As well as Rosie Jones' *Holy Rollers* (2001) and Pat Laughren's *Red Ted And the Great Depression* (1992).

The novel, *33 Postcards From Heaven* was published by Gondwana Press in 2005. Numerous articles, reviews, stories and interviews have been published in *Metro, Cinema Papers, Cantrill's Filmnotes, Australasian Drama Studies, Community Theatre In Australia, The Macquarie Companion to the Australian Media* and *Theatre Research International* (Cambridge University). Paul has also given courses in literature and creative writing at various colleges and universities including: Southern Cross, James Cook and Melbourne State.

FOR CAZ 1951 - 1990